TASTE THE WORLD

with

JENNY MORRIS

TASTE THE WORLD

with

JENNY MORRIS

SUNBIRD PUBLISHERS

博愛

THANK YOU

Taste the World with Jenny Morris is dedicated to my eldest son, Wade Esposito, and to Uncle Tony Esposito, his grandfather, who introduced me to a world of new flavours.

The Moroccan chapter is dedicated with much love to Nick Thorogood from Food Network, UK. Thank you Nick for your gift of a Morocco and its people that I never knew existed; it fed my soul.

The chapter on Borneo is dedicated to my sister Beverley Perold Stephens ... Bev, you know why. Love you!

There are so many special people in my life who have helped to make this book a reality. First, a great big loving "Thank you!" goes to my husband David for always being there for me. And to my sons Darin and Ryan, thanks for being the best sons a mom could wish for.

Thanks to Ana Russo and Susanna Ribeiro, for making me fall in love with Portugal, its food and its people.

To my sweet Ceri Prenter at Sunbird Publishers, thank you and much Jenny love. To my editor, Michelle Marlin, you understand my passion and I love working with you. And to my designer, Marius Roux, you deliver darling.

To my unflappable photographer, Danie Nel – I always love your work! Caro Gardner, I love your passion and your gentle nature. You are a stylish stylist, and it's wonderful having you on board.

Gerrit, I just loved travelling with you and Lesley. Thank you for sharing your beautiful photographs of Morocco with me; I wish I had space for them all.

Many thanks to Moroccan Warehouse for the use of their stunning Moroccan props, and to Breco Seafoods for the supply of their superb seafood.

And to my hard-working staff at the CooksPlayground – you rock!

CONTENTS

FOREWORD

In 1998, when 567 CapeTalk was in its first year of broadcasting, we held a client function at Newlands Rugby Stadium. In place of the predictable canapés and crudités was the most generous, flavourful combination of food I'd ever tasted. That was my introduction to the Giggling Gourmet.

For years after, I had the pleasure of sharing the studio with Jenny on my weekend talk show and I could never have predicted how much fun or how entertaining talking food would be. Along with sharing mouth-watering recipes, Jenny would throw in tips for the romantics. This one I won't forget, "On Valentine's Day, prepare finger foods, run a bubble bath, light candles and put Vaseline on the outside door handle so the kids can't get in."

Jenny started her Cook's Playground at a high school in Cape Town and I remember the first class I attended. Everyone started out wide-eyed and quiet and ended up having to get a taxi home – the wine flowed, we laughed, we stuffed chicken breasts (alcohol-induced bravery), baked our own bread, and made to-die-for dessert. It was the greatest fun I've ever had in front of a stove.

Our Giggling Gourmet has come a long way from having to carry crates of ingredients into the school, opening her own world-class, characterful premises in the upmarket and trendy Cape Quarter situated in the heart of Cape Town.

Jenny makes everyone around her feel special. Her energy and effervescence are boundless and I feel tremendously privileged to have known her from that first event, to watching her star rise and rise.

In 2011, Jenny signed with Food Network, becoming the first South African chef to host her own show on the channel, which is broadcast to the UK, Europe, Middle East, Africa and Asia. Jenny has always said, "I want to taste the world," and now she's sharing her combined love of food and travel with the rest of the world, making everyone who knows her incredibly proud.

Jenny embarked on her Culinary Tours as another way to share her love of exotic tastes, travel and people. I was extremely fortunate to have experienced a journey to Vietnam and Cambodia. We were wined and dined in some of the most upmarket restaurants as well as the humble kitchens of the local people. At each sitting the chefs would talk us through the combination of foods and how they were prepared. We visited the fragrant bustling markets and we had first-hand experience making our own dishes at a cooking school in the ancient town of Hue-An – an absolute must on your travel calendar – and you couldn't wish for better company than our Jen.

My cooking skills are much like the way I play tennis; I'm incredibly enthusiastic, but not very good at it. Yet, I win every time I refer to Jenny's cookbooks – from Pears in Red Wine to Sesame-seared Tuna, I've impressed everyone with the meals I've shared thanks to Jenny. She has the gift of making anyone who finds scrambling an egg a challenge believe that they are a culinary genius – and feel sexy doing it.

David, Jenny's husband, once said that he was battling to get the recipes out of her head, and I'm relieved that he finally succeeded. Here's to another cover-to-cover helping of the most sublime servings.

Charmaine Noy, Radio Presenter, 94.5Kfm

TASTE MY WORLD

Whenever I travel, I come home with my head whirling with new recipes that I just have to try the minute I step back into my own kitchen. I just can't wait to recreate the world of flavours that I encounter in the local markets and the humble kitchens that I so love to visit when I explore a new country.

My luggage is always overweight, full of tasty exotic gifts for friends and family, and I'm devastated by the laws that forbid me to bring certain food products into the country nowadays. I've certainly carried some interesting things across borders in my time. I remember returning from Greece with some sublime thick yoghurt to use as a starter culture so that I could keep on making my own; olives and olive oil (in those days they weren't as readily available as they are now); and sprigs of fragrant herbs. Berries even. I'd buy them in Holland (in those days the only commercial berry available here was a strawberry) and I would cook them and put them in a jar, otherwise they wouldn't last the journey. Wonderful, wonderful halva from Israel. And a 20 kg kabeljou caught and frozen by my friend's husband on a fishing trip to Namibia. It barely fitted into my suitcase and my bag was overweight of course, but I paid the price and brought that fish home.

I also return from my travels with cherished memories of adventures shared with friends old and new – these often lead to a creative burst in my kitchen and a new recipe to try. When we were in Ireland, we visited an organic farm, which had me panting and salivating … row upon row, bed upon bed, field upon field of crisp, beautiful lettuces. There was a journalist with me and I told her, "I am going to eat one of these lettuces right out of the field because it's talking to me, saying 'bite me, bite me', and you have to keep watch." She had to eat it with me, of course, in case we got caught. I wasn't going to jail alone! I've never tasted lettuce like that in my life. We took off its outer leaves, ripped out its little heart and ate it – sheer heaven! Afterwards we took a photograph and you could see we had stolen one because the lettuces were so big and beautiful, and the gap was very obvious. I know it's not nice to steal food when you're in another country but I've carried that stolen lettuce around in my heart ever since. It inspired a salad recipe called My Blue Heaven that I used in my previous book – hearts of crispy iceberg lettuce, crunchy walnuts and a divine blue cheese dressing.

I also remember the fragrance of hot chestnuts roasting beside the road in China; freshly squeezed oranges in Morocco, so bright and sweet it was like drinking liquid sunshine; a ripe French Brie oozing between my fingers that made me squeal with pleasure; the succulent crunchy saltiness of samphire that I tasted for the first time in Ireland. I store all these memories in a flavour bank somewhere in my brain and when I get back home I try to create my interpretation of what I've seen and tasted, and so a new recipe is born.

I am so grateful that I have the opportunity to experience exotic new flavours and to meet the people who create them. But what I love the most is to share my food memories and the recipes I have gleaned from my travels with others.

So close your eyes, don't let anything distract you, and take in all these wonderful flavours and rich aromas. Join me as I taste the world.

Uncle Tony's Kitchen

ITALY

My mouth started to travel at a very young age and it was all thanks to a man called Antonio Esposito. He eventually became my father-in-law and the most wonderful grandfather to my eldest son Wade, but in those days he was known to me simply as Uncle Tony.

He was born in Italy in a little town called Tricase in the province of Lecce. He told me that almost everyone in the town was an Esposito – the butcher, the baker, the barber – and even to this day it would seem that nothing has changed.

His many stories of his home town created in me a wanderlust; I just had to travel to far-off places to taste the world beyond the delicious Italy he had created in my mind.

From the age of 11, while his sons Michael and Alfredo were out surfing, I would sit at Uncle Tony's kitchen table. While he cooked, I would keep him company.

One of my favourite things was this: Uncle Tony would take a thick slice of stale bread (that's the thing about Italians – they never throw away a piece of bread!) and he would rub garlic all over it. Then he'd slice an onion and rub that on the bread, and then do the same thing with a tomato. He'd add a little bit of water, some olive oil and salt – and if you think this is boring you'd better think again. It was utterly delicious and I would devour it straight away, savouring the glorious cooking smells that wafted around me in the kitchen.

How I miss that old man and his cooking.

-SNACK
-PIATTI FREDDI
-BREAKFAST
-COLD DRINKS
-LUNCH
AIR CONDITIONING

The sight of bright-yellow, fleshy, ripe lemons hanging on our lemon trees made Uncle Tony hyperventilate. He taught me that the whole lemon was delicious, and I fell in love with lemon zest the day I first tasted gremolata at his kitchen table.

Seared Tuna Topped with Gremolata, Capers and Rosa Tomatoes

GREMOLATA TOPPING
- ¾ cup roughly chopped Italian parsley
- 2 cloves fresh garlic, crushed
- zest of 1 lemon
- juice of 1½ lemons
- 3 Tbs chopped capers
- 2 spring onions, very thinly sliced
- 1 cup roughly chopped fresh Rosa tomatoes
- salt
- freshly ground pepper
- ½ cup extra virgin olive oil

TUNA
- 4 tuna steaks
- sea salt
- coarsely ground black pepper
- olive oil for frying

Mix all the topping ingredients together before searing the tuna and let it rest until you are ready to serve.

Season the tuna with salt and lots of freshly ground black pepper. Heat the oil in a non-stick frying pan and sear the steaks for a few minutes on each side.

Spoon some gremolata topping over each steak and serve immediately with boiled new potatoes and steamed green beans.

TIP: Tuna should be served rare, and then it will be juicy and succulent; treat it as you would red meat. It is very easy to prepare tuna just the way you like it, as you can watch the colour change as it cooks.

SERVES 4

Uncle Tony's Potato Gnocchi with Rosemary Butter

GNOCCHI

- 1 kg potatoes, washed
- ⅓ cup flour (plus an extra ⅓ cup for later)
- 1 egg yolk
- ½ tsp salt
- a good shake of grated nutmeg

ROSEMARY BUTTER

- 100 g butter
- 2 Tbs fresh rosemary needles
- 2 cloves garlic, finely chopped
- salt
- freshly ground black pepper
- freshly grated Parmesan cheese

Preheat the oven to 200 °C. Uncle Tony used to bake the potatoes to keep them from getting waterlogged. Place the potatoes on a baking tray and cut a slit into each one, then bake them till they are nice and tender when poked. Allow them to cool slightly, cut them in half lengthways and scoop out the warm flesh. Mash it in a bowl until it is smooth.

Add a third of a cup of flour, the egg yolk, salt and nutmeg, and mix lightly together.

Turn the potato dough out onto a well-floured surface, and knead in enough of the extra flour to make a smooth, but not sticky, dough. Divide the dough into four and roll into sausages on a lightly floured surface.

Cut each sausage into bite-sized portions. Press your thumb gently in the centre of each piece to make an indentation to trap the butter.

Gnocchi needs lots of space to cook, so fill a large pot with lots of water, bring to a rolling boil, salt it and, adding only a few at a time, drop the gnocchi into the water for about a minute or until they decide to float to the surface. Remove with a slotted spoon, keep warm and continue until they are all cooked.

Now prepare the rosemary butter. Heat the butter in a large frying pan until it foams. Add the rosemary needles and cook gently till they curl, add the garlic and some salt and pepper to taste. Gently stir in the gnocchi and warm through.

Pile into bowls and top with lots of freshly grated Parmesan.

SERVES 4

I remember how fresh fish and seafood were so abundant when I was growing up. If you felt like eating mussels, you would grab a sack and go down to the beach when the tide was out and pick them fresh off the rocks. Uncle Tony and Alfredo, Wade's dad, would come home laden. We would scrub and clean them, and then Uncle Tony would put them into the biggest pot I have ever seen and steam them open. They were fat, juicy, sweet and succulent – just like mussels should be!

Uncle Tony's Mussels

- 1.5 kg cleaned fresh mussels
- ⅓ cup dry white wine
- ½ cup fresh seawater
- 3 Tbs extra virgin olive oil
- 4 cloves garlic, sliced
- ¾ cup freshly chopped flat leaf parsley
- 1 Tbs butter
- salt
- freshly ground black pepper

Pick the mussels over before you start and throw out any broken ones. Place the mussels in a large saucepan and add the wine, seawater, olive oil and garlic. Cover the pot and steam them for about five minutes or until the shells open.

Remove to a large platter with a slotted spoon, then stir in the parsley and butter, season with salt and pepper, and dig in.

SERVES 4

Salsa Verde

- 2 cloves garlic
- 1 cup flat leaf parsley
- 1 Tbs mint
- 1 Tbs coriander
- 1 Tbs basil
- 1 Tbs chives
- 2 Tbs chopped capers
- 5 anchovy fillets
- 2 tsp Dijon mustard
- ½ cup extra virgin olive oil
- freshly ground black pepper
- 1 Tbs lemon juice
- 1 tsp lemon zest

Uncle Tony would fling together a quick bowl of spaghetti and just stir in a few tablespoons of this delicious Salsa Verde.

Place all the ingredients except the lemon juice and zest into the bowl of your food processor and whizz it a few times to bring it together into a thick paste.

Taste and adjust the seasoning. Add the lemon juice and zest just before stirring it into the cooked pasta.

TIP: The acid from the juice dulls the vibrant green of the herbs so add it at the very last minute.

FOR 4 SERVINGS OF PASTA

My father grew so many lemon trees in our garden and every year we had more fruit than we knew what to do with. We soon started to share our harvest and recipes with friends and in return we sometimes learnt something new to do with the lemons.

That was the case when my father gave Uncle Tony baskets of fragrant sun-ripened lemons. Uncle Tony said that families in Italy have passed down their Limoncello recipe for generations, and every Italian family has its own recipe. He taught Dad how to make his Limoncello. He kept the bottles of delicious lemony syrup in the freezer, and then he would pour it over ice to sip on hot summer nights.

I bottle up a lot of Limoncello. It makes a wonderful gift and nothing gives me more of a kick than when my guests sip my homemade Limoncello and sigh with pleasure as the icy, zesty, sweet boozy lemon syrup slides down their throats.

Limoncello

- 15 unblemished really ripe unwaxed lemons
- 2 × 750 ml bottles vodka
- 5 cups water
- 4 cups sugar

Using a potato peeler, peel the zest thinly off the lemons, taking care not cut any of the pith with the peel as this will result in a very bitter Limoncello.

Place the zest into a large jar with one bottle of vodka and let it macerate for a minimum of six weeks. Yes, let it wallow in the vodka giving up all that wonderful yellow lemon flavour trapped in the skin. I know it is tempting to open the jar and put your nose to that beautiful lemon scent, but don't. Keep it in the jar, and keep the jar out of the sun and in a cool dark place to rest.

After the six weeks are up, it is time to make the syrup. Place the water and sugar in a saucepan and stir until the sugar has dissolved, cooking it gently till it resembles a light syrup. Remove from the heat and cool.

Add the cooled syrup to your lemony vodka, add the remaining bottle of vodka and put it back into hiding for six more weeks.

Strain the zest out of the Limoncello (yes, it is now Limoncello) and bottle. Store the bottles in the freezer and sip the syrup on hot summer nights over ice or after your dinner as a digestive.

TIP: Look for thick-skinned lemons because they have plenty of zest. Most importantly, if the lemons don't come from your tree but are store-bought, wash them thoroughly with a soft brush and hot water to remove any wax, and then rub them dry.

The higher the alcohol content of the vodka, the better – the Limoncello will not turn to ice in the freezer.

MAKES ABOUT 4 BOTTLES

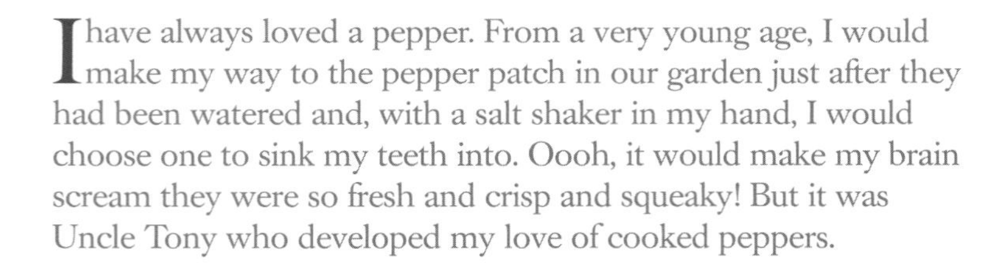
I have always loved a pepper. From a very young age, I would make my way to the pepper patch in our garden just after they had been watered and, with a salt shaker in my hand, I would choose one to sink my teeth into. Oooh, it would make my brain scream they were so fresh and crisp and squeaky! But it was Uncle Tony who developed my love of cooked peppers.

Peperonata

- 5 Tbs olive oil
- 2 red peppers, quartered and deseeded
- 2 orange peppers, quartered and deseeded
- 2 yellow peppers, quartered and deseeded
- 2 green peppers, quartered and deseeded
- 3 cloves garlic, chopped
- 2 red onions, thinly sliced
- 300 g cherry tomatoes, halved
- 3 Tbs balsamic vinegar
- ¾ cup black pitted olives
- 1 tsp thyme leaves
- 1 tsp finely chopped rosemary needles
- salt
- freshly ground black pepper

Heat the oil in a large frying pan, stir fry the peppers and garlic, and cook for 10 minutes. Remove from the pan. Stir the onions into the same pan, cooking gently till they wilt.

Remove from the pan, adding them to the cooled peppers. Then add the tomatoes to the same pan and cook for 10 minutes. Stir in the balsamic vinegar, olives and herbs, and season with salt and pepper. Cook for a minute, stir the mixture into the peppers and cool to room temperature.

TIP: Use the freshest, most unblemished peppers you can find to make this delicious starter. If there is any left, I blitz it in the blender and pull it through pasta, topping it with lots of grated Parmesan and freshly chopped herbs.

SERVES 8

Stuffed Peppers

- 2 Tbs olive oil
- 2 cloves garlic, crushed
- 200 g pancetta, or bacon, chopped
- 1 small onion, chopped
- 2 celery sticks, finely chopped
- 1 cup fresh breadcrumbs
- 2 Tbs basil pesto
- ½ cup flat leaf parsley, chopped
- 300 g ricotta cheese
- salt
- freshly ground black pepper
- 4 large red peppers with stems
- olive oil for drizzling
- grated Parmesan cheese

Preheat the oven to 180 °C. Heat the oil in a large frying pan and gently fry the garlic, pancetta, onion and celery till the onion is translucent. Stir in the breadcrumbs, pesto and parsley. Cool the mixture, stir in the ricotta, and season to taste.

Cut the peppers lengthways through the stalk and gently cut out the pith. Fill with the ricotta mix and drizzle with a little olive oil. Place on a baking tray and bake for 20 to 25 minutes.

Top with some grated Parmesan cheese and bake for a further five minutes. Serve with a very large green salad.

SERVES 4

Italian Bread Tart

BASIC BREAD DOUGH
- 4 cups cake flour
- 2 tsp salt
- 4 tsp sugar
- 10 g instant yeast
- 1 Tbs olive oil (sunflower will do)
- 1½ cups lukewarm water

TOPPING
- 4 garlic cloves, crushed
- 200 g ricotta cheese
- 200 g bocconcini balls
- 40 cherry tomatoes
- salt
- freshly ground black pepper
- olive oil for drizzling
- salsa verde (see page 17)
- shaved Parmesan

This is like a large hot Caprese salad in a bread bowl. It can also be served at room temperature and is great to take along on a picnic.

Preheat the oven to 200 °C. To make the tart bases, place all the dry ingredients for the dough into a bowl and make a well in the centre. Add the oil and three quarters of the water, and mix to form a soft dough. Add a little more water if need be; if it is too wet, add a small amount of flour.

Knead the dough until it is smooth and elastic to the touch; about 15 minutes. Place the dough back into the bowl and oil the top; cover with a clean cloth and place it in a warm place to rise to twice its size.

Once the bread dough has proved, punch it down and divide into six portions. Push or roll each portion into a thin circle and raise the edges slightly to form a lip. Lightly oil the tart bases and place them onto hot, oiled baking trays. Prick the bases with a fork, bake for six minutes, remove from the oven and cool.

Get ready to top the bases. Preheat the oven to 220 °C. Divide the garlic between the bases and spread it thinly over the top. Divide the ricotta, bocconcini and tomatoes onto the bases, squashing the tomatoes into the tart. Season with salt and pepper, and drizzle with a little olive oil.

Bake the tarts for seven to 10 minutes or until the bases are crisp and golden. Spoon over the salsa verde, scatter over some shaved Parmesan and serve.

SERVES 6

Uncle Tony used my parent's garden to plant vegetables and would drop by after work to have a chat to his plants and shower them with love and water. He would pick what he wanted and then make his way home.

Broccoli, Potato and Pine Nut Salad

DRESSING
- ⅔ cup olive oil
- ⅓ cup white wine vinegar
- 1 tsp honey
- 6 spring onions with tops, finely sliced
- 2 cloves peeled garlic
- 1 tsp chopped fresh mint
- salt
- freshly ground black pepper

SALAD
- 200 g long-stemmed broccoli
- 4 large potatoes, peeled
- ½ cup toasted pine nuts
- 1 cup crispy streaky bacon or pancetta, chopped
- handful roughly chopped rocket
- ½ cup roughly chopped Italian parsley

Fling all the dressing ingredients into your liquidiser or food processor and give it a good few whizzes to emulsify. Set aside.

Peel the broccoli stems and steam very lightly. Cool and chop roughly. Boil the potatoes in lightly salted water till just cooked. Strain, cool and slice into rings.

Layer the broccoli in a glass bowl with the potatoes, pine nuts, crispy bacon, rocket, parsley and dressing, and let it stand for a while before serving.

SERVES 6

Once a week my mom used to make crumbed steak, which we loved topped with mustard butter. But along came Uncle Tony and poor Mother's nose was soon out of joint because his veal steaks with lemon caper butter quickly became the firm favourite – as they are to this day!

Lemon and Caper Veal Steaks

- 4 veal or fillet steaks (about 150 g each)
- 1 garlic clove, sliced in half lengthways
- salt
- freshly ground pepper
- paprika
- flour, for dusting
- 1 Tbs olive oil
- 2 Tbs salted butter
- 1 clove garlic, crushed
- 4 Tbs dry white wine
- 1 cup chicken stock
- 4 Tbs lemon juice
- 3 Tbs capers, roughly chopped
- 1 red chilli, chopped
- 2 Tbs flat leaf parsley, chopped
- 1 Tbs chopped chives
- 1 tsp lemon zest
- 1 Tbs butter

Flatten the veal or fillet steaks between two pieces of plastic wrap; rub each steak with the cut side of the garlic. Season the steaks with salt, pepper and paprika, and dust lightly with flour.

Heat the olive oil and butter in a frying pan, and fry the steaks two at a time for a couple of minutes on each side, or until lightly golden.

Remove the steaks and deglaze the pan with the wine. Add the stock and lemon juice, and cook till it is reduced by a third. Stir in the capers and chilli, and cook for two minutes.

Return the steaks to the pan and heat through. Stir in the parsley, chives and lemon zest, and remove from the heat. Taste for seasoning and dot with the remaining butter.

Serve with a Parmesan and herbed polenta, steamed green beans and a salad.

SERVES 4

I just love tomatoes. We grew up with them in our garden and we used them in bredies and stews, salads and jams, but never as a side dish with meat. Uncle Tony taught me how to get the most out of a cooked tomato, how to roast it to intensify the flavour. He also introduced me to capers! Please try this delicious combination.

Rib-eye with Pan-fried Tomatoes and Rosemary Caper Butter

- 4 × 250 – 300 g rib-eye steaks
- 2 Tbs olive oil
- 400 g cherry tomatoes
- 1 Tbs chopped fresh rosemary needles
- 2 cloves garlic, chopped
- 2 Tbs capers, roughly chopped
- salt
- freshly ground black pepper
- 1 Tbs butter
- zest of 1 lemon
- 1 Tbs chopped flat leaf parsley
- grated Parmesan

Leave the steaks out of the fridge until you are ready to cook them – they should be at room temperature.

Heat the olive oil in a large frying pan and add the tomatoes, cooking them till the skins burst. Add the rosemary, garlic and capers, and cook for six minutes. Season with salt and pepper, stir in the butter and lemon zest, and cook for a minute. Stir in the parsley and set aside while you cook the steaks.

Season the steaks and fry them in a really hot pan to the way you like them – I like mine medium-rare. Keep them warm while you reheat the tomatoes.

Place the steaks onto warmed plates, top with tomatoes and a dusting of freshly grated Parmesan, and serve with a rocket salad.

TIP: This is delicious served with polenta.

SERVES 4

Chicken Tonnato

CHICKEN
- 2 cups dry white wine
- 2 cups chicken stock
- 3 cloves garlic
- 1 onion, thickly sliced
- 1 large carrot, peeled and roughly chopped
- 1 large celery rib, roughly chopped
- 2 fresh bay leaves
- 3 dried cloves
- 12 peppercorns
- peel (without any pith) from a ripe lemon
- 6 large skinless chicken breasts on the bone

TONNATO SAUCE
- 100 g tuna chunks in oil
- 14 anchovy fillets
- 4 parsley stalks
- 2 fresh egg yolks
- 2 Tbs lemon juice (from a very ripe lemon)
- ½ cup extra virgin olive oil
- salt
- freshly ground black pepper

GARNISH
- fresh parsley, chopped
- 3 Tbs capers
- zest of 1 lemon
- freshly ground black pepper

Alma Morris, this is for you! I ate this delicious chicken and tuna dish for the first time at the table of Tony Esposito – a first for me to eat fish and poultry together – and my mouth fell in love with it. My mother-in-law Alma made her own delicious version of it, and this is mine.

Place the wine in a saucepan with the stock, garlic, onion, carrot, celery, bay leaves, cloves, peppercorns and lemon peel. Bring to the boil.

Place the chicken breasts bone-side down into the stock, bring back to the boil, turn down the heat, cover and simmer for 25 minutes.

Remove from the heat and let the chicken stand in the stock for a further five minutes. Remove the chicken and let it cool.

Strain the sauce and return to the pot. Simmer till it has reduced to more or less one cup, then remove from the heat.

To make the sauce, place the tuna with its oil, the anchovies and the parsley stalks in a blender and give it a whizz. Add the egg yolks with one tablespoon of lemon juice, whizz again until smooth. Now, with the motor running, slowly add the olive oil, and once it is incorporated slowly add the stock. Adjust the seasoning and top up the lemon juice if the sauce needs it.

Time to plate it! Slice the chicken thinly off the bone and overlap the slices on a platter. Spoon over the sauce and garnish with the parsley, capers and lemon zest. Finish with a grind of black pepper.

Serve with a huge bowl of green salad leaves topped with sliced red onions.

SERVES 6

I loved the aromas that came from Uncle Tony's kitchen. While I helped him slice tomatoes to sun dry on his porch, he used to tell me stories of how his mother did the same when he was growing up. He said he could still taste that intense tomato flavour in his mind.

Aromatic Tomato and Chicken Pasta Lunch

AROMATIC TOMATO PASTE

- 2 Tbs toasted coriander seeds
- 1 Tbs toasted cumin seeds
- 3 cloves garlic, crushed
- 2 Tbs olive oil
- 1 dried chilli
- 2 × 400 g cans tomatoes, chopped
- ½ tsp ground cinnamon
- salt
- black pepper
- handful Italian parsley, chopped
- handful coriander, chopped

CHICKEN PASTA

- olive oil
- 4 chicken breasts, cut into bite-sized pieces
- 6 spring onions with tops, chopped
- 1 red pepper, chopped
- 2 celery ribs, sliced
- 2 cloves garlic, chopped
- salt
- freshly ground black pepper
- 1 Tbs capers
- ½ cup chopped black olives
- 1 quantity aromatic tomato paste
- 4 cups cooked penne pasta
- Parmesan cheese
- freshly chopped parsley

Pound the coriander, cumin, garlic and a tablespoon of olive oil together to a paste. Heat the remaining oil in a pan, add the chilli and gently fry the paste until the aromatic fragrance of the spices wafts off the pan – don't burn it.

Add the tomatoes and cinnamon, and cook gently till thick and chunky. Season with salt and pepper, stir in the chopped parsley and coriander, and set aside.

To make the pasta, heat the oil in a saucepan, add the chicken and cook for five minutes. Add the spring onions, red pepper, celery and garlic. Cook, stirring for six minutes. Season to taste.

Now add the capers, olives and aromatic tomato paste, and cook very gently for 10 minutes. Stir in the pasta and heat through.

Spoon into bowls, dust with lots of grated Parmesan and a scattering of freshly chopped parsley.

SERVES 4 TO 6

Uncle Tony always spoke about how his mother would make a tart with whatever fruit was in season – he especially loved her grape and pear tarts. She would always put almonds into her pastry, which would sometimes be used to make little cookies with a whole almond pressed into the top. I have continued the tradition.

Almond, Orange and Pear Tart

PASTRY

- ¾ cup flour
- 50 g ground almonds
- ¼ cup castor sugar
- 1 tsp finely grated orange zest
- 60 g chilled butter, cut into little cubes
- 1 egg yolk, beaten
- 2–3 Tbs iced water

FILLING

- 125 g mascarpone
- ¼ cup sugar
- 1 egg
- ½ tsp vanilla extract
- 1 Tbs flour
- 1 Tbs ground almonds
- 3 Tbs milk

PEAR TOPPING

- 4 pears, peeled, cored and quartered
- juice of ½ orange
- 50 g almonds, roughly chopped
- 1 Tbs honey
- 1 Tbs castor sugar
- 1 Tbs orange marmalade
- 1 Tbs almond or orange liqueur

To make the pastry, place the flour, ground almonds, castor sugar and orange zest into a bowl, and mix well. Scatter the cubed butter onto the flour and, with cool fingertips, rub together until the mixture resembles fine breadcrumbs. Stir in the egg and enough water to bring the dough together – not too sticky.

Lightly flour a clean surface and knead the dough with cool hands till smooth. Wrap the dough in cling wrap and chill for 30 minutes.

Preheat the oven to 190 °C. Roll the pastry out to fit a 23 cm loose-bottomed tart tin. Line with greaseproof paper and pour in enough dry beans to cover the base of the tin. Bake the pastry blind for 10 minutes, then remove the paper and beans and set aside the tart crust to cool completely.

To make the filling, place the mascarpone, sugar, egg, vanilla, flour and almonds into a bowl, and stir in the milk, blending till smooth. Spread onto the base of the cooled pastry shell.

To make the topping, toss the peeled pears in the orange juice. Now arrange the pears on the pastry base, pointed ends meeting in the centre. Scatter over the nuts, drizzle with honey and sprinkle over the castor sugar. Bake at 190 °C for 40 to 45 minutes or until the pears are tender and the filling is set.

Warm the marmalade and liqueur together, and when the marmalade has melted brush it over the warm pears. Serve with freshly whipped cream.

SERVES 4 TO 6

Uncle Tony used to brew coffee on the stove and never wasted a drop – it sometimes became the dipping mixture for tiramisu, such a delicious dessert that I first tasted in his kitchen. I like the idea of a lovely summer fruit one, so I make this tasty version a lot when berries are in season and then I ask his forgiveness for what I have done.

Summer Berry Tiramisu

- 5 eggs, separated
- ¾ cup castor sugar
- 300 g mascarpone cheese
- 1 cup cranberry or berry juice
- 3 Tbs Cointreau
- 36 ginger biscuits
- 3 cups raspberries, puréed
- 100 g dark chocolate, for grating
- fresh raspberries, for garnishing

Beat the egg yolks and sugar together until light and fluffy. Add the mascarpone and beat until smooth.

In a very clean bowl, whisk the egg whites till soft peak stage and fold gently into the mascarpone mix.

Mix the juice with the Cointreau in a shallow dish, dip the biscuits into the juice mixture and make a layer on the base of a 25 cm dish. Spread half the berry purée onto the biscuits, and then top with half the mascarpone mixture.

Soak the remaining biscuits and continue to layer as before, ending with the mascarpone. Cover and chill for several hours.

Dust with grated chocolate and dot with fresh raspberries just before serving.

SERVES 4 TO 6

When I was in Lisbon to launch my Food Network television programme *Jenny Morris Cooks Morocco* I was lucky enough to meet Ana Russo. Not only does she head up a company that represents the local cable network station, she is also an acclaimed photographer, homemaker and a woman who is passionate about growing her own food and cooking it. She was the best food guide to Lisbon I could have hoped for!

After a really delicious dinner in the harbour, Ana took us back to the hotel. Making plans for the next day, she said that she would take me to her local fresh fish and vegetable market before we went to lunch. I was really excited at the prospect of a visit to the market and could hardly wait.

She arrived nice and early to collect me so that I would not miss a thing. Because the housewives shopped early, she wanted to make sure that the stalls would still be full when we arrived. And, my goodness, so they were! There were ice-covered tiled slabs piled with octopus, squid, clams, mussels, prawns and shrimps. Every kind of fish was on display – fish so fresh I swear they were still twitching. Ana had her favourite fishmonger who knew exactly kind of fish she liked, and she placed her order for Monday. But I wanted one for lunch, for today. Now!

I couldn't get enough of that beautiful market with its stalls overflowing with the freshest misshapen organic fruits and vegetables. There were big bunches of fresh thyme and fragrant oregano; garlands of onions and garlic hanging above the stalls; freshly baked crusty rounds of Portuguese bread; mounds of every kind of sausage, salami and chorizo; and piles of wonderful handmade cheeses. Oh, my aching mouth! I had to buy something, I had to cook!

I begged Ana if I could cook lunch for her at her house. I think she saw the desperation in my eyes and she gave in. And so, we started to shop.

22
BATALHA
218
P

The saddest thing I never did was not to buy a kale shredder while I was in Portugal. I am in love with the thread-thin pieces of kale that float in the simple but ever-so-delicious potato-based soup.

When I went to Ana's country house I almost fainted when I saw the giant leafy kale bordering her beautiful, abundant vegetable garden. I had never seen anything like those massive, lush, dark green leaves growing high on their long trunks. Oh, heavens, I just wanted to cook. But more than anything, I wanted to own those plants. I had to get some seeds. I was driven almost to the edge of insanity; I just had to have them. I will say no more for fear of being locked up …

Caldo Verde

- 2 Tbs olive oil
- 3 onions, thinly sliced
- 3 cloves garlic, chopped
- ½ tsp salt
- 8 cups chicken or vegetable stock
- 800 g potatoes, peeled and cubed
- 2 fresh bay leaves
- 300 g kale or Savoy cabbage
- 100 g chorizo cut into thin slices
- 1 extra potato, boiled, peeled and cubed
- 1 small red chilli, seeded and diced (optional)
- ground white pepper, to taste

Heat the olive oil in a large saucepan and gently, without browning, cook the onions and garlic with half a teaspoon of salt until they become tender. Add a few tablespoons of stock to stop them sticking, and don't let this burn, okay!

Now it's time to add the potatoes to the pot with a cup of the stock. Stir it around and loosen any onion on the base of the pot. Add the bay leaves and the remaining stock, and simmer gently till the potatoes are soft and fluffy.

Prepare your kale while the soup simmers. Remove the tough stems and then roll the leaves into cigars and slowly and patiently, with a sharp knife, slice the leaves as close to thread-thin as you can.

Heat three cups of water in a saucepan and when it comes to the boil add the kale or cabbage and cook for eight to 10 minutes. Remove the kale and drain it in a colander, but do not throw the cooking water away – you will need it to thin the soup later.

Remove the bay leaves and liquidise the soup with a cup of the cabbage water. Return the soup to the saucepan with another cup of cabbage water, the sliced chorizo and the extra cubed potato. Bring it to the boil and simmer for five minutes.

Stir in the kale and chilli, and add some white pepper to taste. Simmer till the kale is heated through and then spoon into bowls and serve.

TIP: I don't add salt to the cooking water for the kale because there are already salty ingredients in the soup.

SERVES JUST ME, OR 4 TO 6

Susanna Ribeiro told me that in Portugal they say it takes three mad people to make a salad: one to place the ingredients in the bowl; one to makè a dressing; and one to toss it. So, this salad is for Ana, Theresa and Susanna!

Warm Chickpea and Chicken Liver Salad

THE DRESSING
- 2 Tbs red wine vinegar
- 1 tsp dried oregano
- 1 clove garlic, crushed
- salt, to taste
- 1 tsp hot mustard powder
- 5 Tbs olive oil

THE SALAD
- 2 Tbs olive oil
- 150 g chorizo, chopped
- 1 red pepper, diced
- 2 cloves garlic, crushed
- 1 Tbs red wine vinegar
- 2 cups chickpeas, cooked
- ½ cup chopped parsley
- salt and pepper, to taste
- rocket or cos lettuce
- chopped parsley, to garnish

THE LIVERS
- ½ cup sifted flour
- ¼ cup cornflour
- salt and pepper, to taste
- 1 tsp paprika
- ½ tsp chilli powder
- 500 g chicken livers, cleaned and dried
- olive oil for frying

In a screw-top jar, mix together the vinegar, oregano, garlic, salt and mustard powder, stirring well to dissolve the mustard. Add the olive oil and give it a good shake.

Now let's make the salad. Heat the oil in a frying pan and add the chorizo. Fry till crisp, add the red pepper and cook stirring for two minutes. Add the garlic, cook for about half a minute, stir in the vinegar and cook for another minute. Add the chickpeas and parsley, season with salt and pepper and leave to cool while you prepare the livers.

Mix the flours with the seasoning and spices and roll the livers in it, shaking off the excess. Heat the oil and fry the livers in batches till golden and slightly pink inside.

To assemble the salad, pile the cooled chickpea mixture onto a bed of rocket or cos lettuce, top with the chicken livers, spoon over the dressing, and scatter with some chopped parsley to finish it off.

SERVES 4

Ana's Soupy Fish Pasta

- 4 Tbs olive oil
- 2 onions, chopped
- 2 carrots, chopped
- 1 fennel bulb, thinly sliced
- 2 sticks celery, thinly sliced
- 2 fresh bay leaves
- 3 cloves garlic, crushed
- 6 large tomatoes, grated
- 5 cups chicken stock
- ¾ cup white wine
- salt
- freshly ground black pepper
- 2 cups raw macaroni, or similar pasta shapes
- 6 thick, firm, white fish cutlets, skin on
- flat leaf parsley, chopped

This is a meal I ate at Ana's home. It was a bowl of pure comfort!

Heat the oil and gently fry the onions, carrots, fennel, celery, bay leaves and garlic for about five minutes. Add the tomatoes and cook for three minutes.

Add the stock and wine and season with salt and pepper. Cook for 20 minutes. Add the macaroni and fish, and cook till the pasta is tender and the fish cooked through.

Stir in the parsley and serve in deep bowls.

SERVES 4 TO 6

Very-peri Buttered Prawns

- 24 king prawns, deveined

PERI-PERI BUTTER
- 150 g salted butter
- 6 cloves garlic, crushed
- 2 tsp grated fresh ginger
- 3 Tbs lemon juice
- zest of 1 very ripe lemon
- 1 tsp dried oregano
- 3 red chillies
- ¼ tsp ground white pepper
- 1 Tbs fresh rosemary needles, roughly chopped
- 1 Tbs chopped fresh coriander
- ½ cup olive oil
- 1 tsp salt

THE RICE
- 2 Tbs butter
- 3 spring onions with tops, thinly sliced
- ½ glass white wine
- 3 cups cooked rice
- 2 Tbs chopped parsley

The firm flesh of the prawns, covered in this chilli herby buttery sauce, and a large chunk of freshly baked bread to mop up the juices is all you need – you will be in heaven.

Devein the prawns, trim the feelers and butterfly them, keeping the shell on.

Place the ingredients for the peri-peri butter into the bowl of a food processor and blend together quickly.

Heat half the peri-peri butter in a large heavy pan, and add half the prepared prawns. Cook till all traces of grey are gone and set aside, keeping them warm. Add the remaining butter to the pan and cook the rest of the prawns in the same way.

Make the rice now, placing the butter in the same pan you used for the prawns. Stir in the spring onions and wine, and bring to the boil. Add the rice and heat through. Stir in the parsley and serve with the prawns and big mixed salad.

SERVES 4

I met the beautiful young Igor Martinho, voted Chef of the Year in 2011, when I was in Portugal to launch my Food Network television series *Jenny Morris Cooks Morocco.* He invited us to have Sunday lunch at his family's café in the village of Arrouquelas.

We started with a deliciously fresh soft, sweet creamy cheese (which is a little like ricotta) seasoned with salt and pepper and drizzled with olive oil. There was also a plate of sliced sheep's cheese, which was dry and salty and filled my mouth with flavour; and then bowls of locally cured olives; deep-fried mackerel; a creamy tomato rice, which had such a wonderful texture – perfect for risotto – but sadly grows only in Portugal; a salad of grilled pig's ear with garlic, red wine vinegar, olive oil and fresh coriander, and chunks of fragrant bread baked in a wood oven, all washed down with glasses of chilled Guarda Rios Rosé.

Then like magic appeared octopus, cooked in butter and olive oil with garlic, fresh coriander, lemon juice and a good shake of smoked paprika. Not to mention the potatoes freshly dug from Igor's father's garden. Then there were clams with more chunks of toasted bread drenched in olive oil. I ate so many octopus and clams dishes while I was in Lisbon that I was hooked.

Chilli Clams and Squid Heads

THE CLAMS
- ½ cup olive oil
- 1 stick celery, sliced
- 3 cloves garlic, sliced
- 1 large red chilli
- 1 fresh bay leaf
- 4 cups large clams in their shells, cleaned
- 1 cup dry white wine
- juice of 1 lemon
- 1 Tbs butter
- salt and freshly ground black pepper
- 1 Tbs chopped coriander
- 2 Tbs chopped flat leaf parsley

THE SQUID
- 1 kg cleaned squid heads
- salt and pepper, to taste
- cornflour
- oil for deep frying
- freshly chopped parsley
- paprika

Heat the oil in a saucepan large enough to hold the clams, and add the celery, garlic, chilli and bay leaf. Cook gently till the celery softens a little.

Add the wine and bring to the boil, then add the clams and give the pot a good shake. Cover and cook till the shells open, discarding any unopened clams as they are not good to eat.

Add the lemon juice and butter, season with salt and pepper, and stir in the coriander and parsley. Set aside while you prepare the squid heads.

Make sure that the squid is dry, then season with salt and pepper, and dust with cornflour. Heat the oil and fry the squid heads in small batches, and drain on paper towels.

To serve, spoon the clams into a platter with a lip to hold the sauce, top with the squid, scatter with parsley and shower with a little paprika. Serve with chunks of cucumber and black olives dressed with oregano, olive oil and lemon juice, and a bowl of crusty bread.

SERVES 4

When Ana took me to her local market, I first bought a beautiful, big orange fish. Then came the herbs, garlic, salad ingredients, fresh figs and peaches, bread and cheese, as well as bunches of gorgeous flowers for Ana and Susanna from the old flower seller. This old lady had apparently been selling flowers for 74 years, starting when she was 10 years old. It made me sad to see this 84-year-old still working, but she seemed to be really happy surrounded by her flowers.

With enough food to feed 20 people we made our way to Ana's apartment to cook lunch. Ana had just harvested some beautiful red potatoes from the garden of her country house, so they had to be part of the dish.

Whole Baked Fish with New Potatoes

- 500 g par-boiled new potatoes, halved
- 2 onions, thinly sliced
- 3 tomatoes, thinly sliced
- 4 cloves garlic, thinly sliced
- 2 fresh bay leaves
- salt and pepper, to taste
- 3 Tbs olive oil
- 1 cup dry white wine
- 1 whole firm-fleshed fish (2 kg) or 4 small ones
- ½ cup chopped flat leaf parsley

Preheat the oven to 200 °C. Place the potatoes on the base of a baking dish with the onions, tomatoes, garlic and bay leaves. Season with salt and pepper and drizzle with two tablespoons of olive oil and half the white wine. Toss together and bake for 10 minutes. Remove from the oven and prepare the fish.

Wash and dry the fish and make three slashes into the flesh. Remove a third of the tomato mixture, without potatoes, from the baking dish and set aside.

Season the fish and place it on top of the remaining tomato mixture in the baking dish. Pour over the rest of the white wine and olive oil, and spread the reserved tomato mix onto the fish.

Reduce the oven temperature to 180 °C and bake for 20 to 25 minutes, or until the fish is succulent and flaking from the bone. Whatever you do, don't overcook it!

Scatter the fish with chopped parsley and bring it to the table in the baking dish or placed on a platter. Serve with a gloriously abundant green salad and Portuguese rolls for mopping up the sauce, and a few bottles of chilled, fruity dry white wine.

SERVES 4 TO 6

On the way to Ana's country house we stopped at a field of oregano growing happy and wild. Woody stalks topped with aromatic clumps of leaves and flowers, I smelt its peppery fragrance miles away before I saw it. I couldn't contain my shrieks – what a scent and what a sight to behold. All I wanted to do was roll around in it and cook with it!

Paprika Pork

- 3 Tbs olive oil
- 1½ kg pork neck, cubed
- 2 large onions, chopped
- 2 sticks celery, sliced
- 1 red chilli, chopped
- 2 tsp paprika
- 3 cloves garlic, crushed
- 1 large fresh bay leaf
- 1 tsp dried oregano
- 1 Tbs tomato purée
- 2 cups chicken stock
- 1 cup pre-soaked white beans
- freshly ground black pepper
- 1 cup white wine
- salt
- ½ cup parsley, chopped

I love hearty, rustic Portuguese stews – a pig's trotter would enrich this dish and make it all sticky and yummy. I dare you – add more!

Heat the oil in a saucepan and brown the pork in batches; remove and set aside.

Add more oil to the saucepan if needed, and fry the onions and celery till translucent. Stir in the chilli, paprika, garlic, bay leaf, oregano and tomato purée, and cook for a minute. Stir in the pork and add the stock and beans, and season with pepper.

Cook gently till the beans soften, and then add the wine and salt to taste. Simmer for 15 minutes. Stir in the parsley and serve with boiled parsley potatoes.

TIP: If you add salt at the beginning of the cooking process, the beans will not soften.

SERVES 4 TO 6

In Lisbon, my day begins with delicious soft fried eggs. Their trembling yolks are so orange it looks like the sun is smiling up from my plate. They come served with a sprinkle of oregano and cracked pink peppercorns, and delicious garlicky peppery salami and sausages, and bacon thinly sliced from the pork belly and fried so crisp it looks like lace. And delicious handmade local breads and cheeses – what a way to start the day.

And the tarts! Pastry so crisp it shatters as you bite into it and the creamy-rich eggy custard just wobbles into your mouth. Platters of gorgeous sliced chocolate and fruit sponges rich with enough egg yolk to stop your heart, I am sure. There are always three different loaf cakes, based on the deliciously dense Madeira cake. I develop an especially good relationship with the one that is infused with orange and has bits of chopped glacé fruit stirred through it.

Madeira Cake

THE CAKE

- 250 g unsalted butter
- 1 cup castor sugar
- 4 eggs
- 1 tsp vanilla extract
- 1 Tbs orange zest
- 1½ cups sifted flour
- pinch of salt
- 1½ tsp baking powder
- 3 Tbs natural yoghurt or milk
- juice of 1 large orange
- ¾ cup finely chopped glacé fruit (optional)

LEMON GLAZE

- ⅓ cup lemon juice (juice of about 1½ lemons)
- 3 Tbs fresh orange juice
- 350 g icing sugar, sifted

Preheat the oven to 180 °C. Prepare a 30 cm × 11 cm loaf tin by buttering a piece of greaseproof paper for the base. Butter the sides and dust with flour so the cake doesn't stick (or you can spray with a non-stick cooking spray), but keep the paper in the base.

Cream the butter and sugar together till it is light and fluffy. Beat in the eggs one at a time until well incorporated, and stir in the vanilla and orange zest.

Mix the flour, salt and baking powder together and sift it into the butter mixture. Stir the yoghurt and orange juice together, and pour it into the butter mixture, stirring well. Gently mix in the glacé fruit.

Spoon into the buttered loaf tin and bake on the middle shelf for 50 to 55 minutes, or until a skewer inserted into the centre comes out clean.

Remove from the oven and after about eight minutes tip the cake out onto a cooling rack to cool completely. Mix all the glaze ingredients together in a small bowl until it has reached the consistency of slightly thickened cream. Pour most of the glaze over the cooled Madeira cake, covering the surface and letting it drip down the sides. When it is dry you can pour over another coat.

I find that Madeira cake tastes better the day after it has been baked, so I generally make it a day before I need it.

TIP: Make sure the butter is at room temperature – it will cream quickly. Lightly flour the glacé fruit so that it doesn't sink to the bottom of the loaf tin.

MAKES 1 CAKE

Baked Custards in Caramel Sauce

THE CARAMEL SAUCE
- ⅔ cup castor sugar
- ¼ cup water

THE CUSTARD
- ¾ cup milk
- ¾ cup single cream
- 1 tsp orange zest
- 2 whole eggs
- 4 extra egg yolks
- ⅓ cup castor sugar
- 2 tsp vanilla extract
- orange zest, to garnish

I had these irresistible baked egg custards for breakfast every morning … and then made sure I walked them off.

Place the sugar and water in a small saucepan and stir over a medium heat until the sugar has dissolved. Now, bring to a gentle boil and cook for about eight minutes without stirring or until the mixture is a good, golden caramel colour – not too dark now, or it will become bitter.

Pour the caramel into four oven-proof ramekins that can hold about 180 ml each. Leave the caramel to cool and set while you prepare the custard.

To make the custard, preheat the oven to 150 °C. Pour the milk and cream into a saucepan and gently bring just to a boil on a medium heat. Stir in the orange zest and remove from the heat immediately.

Whisk the eggs, extra yolks, castor sugar and vanilla in a bowl until well combined. Now gradually add the warm milk and cream, giving it a good whisk to combine. Strain the mixture into a jug and pour into the ramekins.

Place a kitchen towel onto the base of a baking dish big enough to hold the caramels (this keeps them grounded and prevents them from sliding around). Now pour boiling water into the dish to reach halfway up the sides of the ramekins.

Bake for 35 minutes, or until they have set. Remove the ramekins from the oven and cool them down before placing them in the refrigerator until they are nice and cold.

About 30 minutes before you are ready to serve, turn them out onto plates with a little lip to contain the sauce. Garnish with a sprinkling of orange zest.

SERVES 6

SPAIN

I combined my honeymoon with a business trip to Spain, and it was the most delicious time ever.

Our Spanish client was a passionate foodie and all he wanted to do was to have meetings over unforgettable meals. He was so proud of his country's cuisine that he just wanted to fill us up with delicious food.

We quenched our thirst daily from chilled jugs of fruity spiced sangria, and nibbled on tapas that were the highlight of my trip; there was no end to these mouth-watering morsels and so many to choose from that I must have gained at least ten kilos just from eating the tapas alone. There were slices of air-dried jamón; my first taste ever of smoked paprika; huge firm fleshy green olives; sardines served fresh and grilled, or pickled and even smoked. Then there were little dishes of salty anchovies swimming in olive oil; all the succulent prawns, mussels, octopus and clams that are so abundant on the Spanish coast; and delicious saffron-infused paella. And my most favourite of all – smoky, spicy chorizo.

Oh that chorizo! I fell in love with the first mouthful and was smitten. Just the tiniest bit of this gorgeous sausage can transform a dish or make a meal out of nothing, and I just love the spicy oil that oozes out of it when the heat gets to it. It is glorious stirred into eggs, fried potatoes, savoury rice or pasta. In Spain it makes an appearance in so many dishes and in honour of that I always have some in my fridge and freezer. It is the first thing I look for at a farmer's market; homemade and delicious, it's got to be smoky and rich in flavour and deep in colour from the paprika.

I really loved the relaxed lifestyle of the Spanish people. You could just see the passion in their food – all prepared from proudly Spanish seasonal produce, and so fresh that you could taste the sunshine.

PASAGE DE LA PAZ

Hake with Capers and White Bean Mash

HAKE
- 4 × thick hake portions (300 g each)
- salt
- freshly ground black pepper
- flour, for dusting
- olive oil for shallow frying

CAPERS AND TOMATOES
- 3 Tbs capers
- 2 Tbs extra virgin olive oil
- 2 tomatoes, deseeded and diced
- 1 Tbs chopped fresh dill
- juice and finely grated zest of a very large, ripe lemon
- 1 clove garlic, crushed
- salt and pepper, to taste

WHITE BEAN MASH
- 2 Tbs olive oil
- 1 fresh bay leaf
- 2 cloves fresh garlic, chopped
- 1 chopped red chilli
- ½ tsp dried oregano
- ½ tsp paprika
- 2 cans cannellini beans, drained
- 2 Tbs chopped flat leaf parsley
- extra olive oil for drizzling

Freshly fried hake just loves to be in the company of rosy, sun-ripe diced tomato dressed with fresh dill, lemon zest, olive oil and garlic, and served on a bed of white bean mash. You can pre-soak some dried beans overnight if you wish, or you can use them from the can; no shame in that, they just get to your mouth quicker.

Season the fish with salt and pepper and dust lightly with flour. Heat a little olive oil in a frying pan and fry the hake for a few minutes on each side till done.

To make the capers and tomatoes, squeeze the water from the capers and toss them into a hot pan with half a tablespoon of olive oil to crisp. Stir the capers into the remaining ingredients, and set aside.

To make the mash, heat the olive oil in a saucepan and add the bay leaf, garlic, chilli, oregano and paprika. Stir for a minute or so, then stir in the beans and heat through. Stir in the parsley when the beans are warm, and give them a rough mash. Drizzle with a little olive oil.

To serve, pile the mash onto a plate with the hake and spoon over the caper and tomato mixture.

TIP: I sometimes add half a cup of chopped chorizo to the saucepan and fry it up with the garlic; it is quite delicious with the beans.

SERVES 4

Baked Artichoke Bottoms

- 1 Tbs olive oil
- ½ cup chopped chorizo
- 1 small red onion, finely diced
- 2 cloves garlic, finely chopped
- 1 small green pepper, finely chopped
- 1 cup cooked rice
- 1 ripe firm tomato, diced
- 12 green olives, chopped
- 2 Tbs freshly chopped dill
- zest and juice of 1 ripe lemon
- salt
- freshly ground black pepper
- 2 Tbs grated Parmesan cheese
- 1 Tbs chopped fresh parsley
- 8 canned artichoke bottoms

The Spanish just love artichokes – they are grown all over Spain and served in many different ways.

Preheat the oven to 180 °C. Heat the olive oil in a heavy-based frying pan, add the chorizo and cook out the oil. Stir in the onion, garlic and green pepper, and cook stirring for six minutes. Add the rice, tomatoes and olives, and cook stirring for three minutes. Remove from the heat.

Stir in the dill, lemon zest and juice, season with salt and pepper, and stir in the cheese and parsley. Fill the artichoke bottoms with the rice mixture, place on a baking tray, drizzle with olive oil and bake for 20 minutes.

Serve with a large green salad and a grating of Parmesan.

SERVES 4

Artichoke and Potato Cakes

- 1 Tbs olive oil
- 2 Tbs finely diced red pepper
- 2 cloves garlic, crushed
- 3 Tbs diced black olives
- 1 small red onion, finely chopped
- 2 Tbs chopped flat leaf parsley
- 500 g potatoes, cooked and mashed
- 1 × 400 g can artichoke bottoms, drained and finely chopped
- ¾ cup grated Parmesan cheese
- salt
- freshly ground black pepper
- 1 large egg, beaten
- flour, for dusting
- oil, for frying

I just love these delicious little cakes; I serve them as part of a tapas starter.

Heat the olive oil in a frying pan and very gently, without browning, cook the red pepper, garlic, olives and red onion for two minutes. Remove from the heat and cool.

In a bowl place the cooled onion mix, parsley, mashed potato, artichokes and Parmesan cheese. Season with salt and pepper to taste, and mix together with the beaten egg.

Shape the mixture into cakes, roll in flour and chill for 30 minutes. Heat some oil in a pan and fry the cakes till golden on both sides. Drain on paper towels and serve immediately.

SERVES 4

When I think of my time in Spain, I remember oranges and olives, chilly sips of sherry, whole roasted baby lamb, delicious figs and chunks of cheese. Oh, there were so many wonderful ingredients that I wanted to gather up and begin to cook then and there, but I was on honeymoon and should not have been thinking about food!

Chicken and Sultanas with Toasted Pine Nuts

- 8 mixed chicken portions
- salt
- freshly ground black pepper
- 2 Tbs olive oil
- 1 large onion, thinly sliced
- 4 cloves garlic, crushed
- 1 green pepper, cut into strips
- 1 × 400 g canned tomatoes
- ¾ cup white wine
- 1 bay leaf
- ½ cup green olives, pitted
- 4 Tbs sultanas
- 2 Tbs toasted pine nuts
- fresh parsley, chopped

Season the chicken with salt and pepper. Heat the oil in a saucepan and brown the chicken pieces – remove and set aside till needed.

In the same saucepan fry the onion, garlic and green pepper till translucent. Add the tomatoes, wine and bay leaf, and simmer for five minutes. Return the chicken to the pot and stir in the olives and sultanas. Simmer gently till the chicken is cooked and tender; about 45 minutes.

Place the chicken in a serving dish, spoon over the sauce, top with pine nuts and parsley and serve.

SERVES 4

Potato, Pepper and Chicken Tortilla

- 1 Tbs olive oil
- 1 onion, thinly sliced
- ¾ cup diced spicy chorizo sausage
- 300 g potatoes, finely diced
- 1 cup diced chicken breast fillet
- 2 cloves garlic, crushed
- 1 large red pepper, diced
- 3 Tbs roughly chopped flat leaf parsley
- salt and freshly ground black pepper
- 10 eggs, beaten
- ½ cup cream

Preheat the oven to 180 °C. Heat the oil in a large frying pan that can go into the oven, and add the onion, stirring for a minute. Stir in the chorizo, cook for two minutes, and stir in the potatoes, cooking till almost tender.

In a separate pan heat a little olive oil and gently fry the chicken, garlic and red pepper together for five minutes. Stir in the parsley and add the mixture to the potatoes. Mix well, and season with salt and pepper.

Stir the eggs and cream together, mixing thoroughly, and pour over the potato mixture. Give it a gentle stir to mix the egg in.

Keeping the heat low, gently cook for about eight minutes to set the base, and then place the pan in the oven and cook for about 20 minutes until the tortilla is set and golden brown.

Remove from the oven and rest for a few minutes before sliding the tortilla gently from the pan.

Serve warm or at room temperature with a beautiful big Spanish-inspired Jenny salad (see page 63).

SERVES 6

Ha! Those short Spanish men just drove me crazy with all the attention they gave me. Manolo, our Spanish client, said that if I had not already been snapped up, I would have landed a Spanish husband in next to no time. But, I would have had to be able to knock up this hearty dish, which is a standby in any Spanish home!

Chicken, Chorizo and Olive Stew

- 12 chicken thighs
- salt and freshly ground black pepper
- 1 Tbs olive oil
- 2 onions, chopped
- 2 sticks celery, chopped
- ½ cup chorizo, finely chopped
- 4 cloves garlic, crushed
- 1 large red pepper, diced
- 2 fresh bay leaves
- 1 tsp smoked paprika
- 4 Tbs raisins
- 4 large ripe tomatoes, chopped
- 1 Tbs tomato purée
- ½ cup medium sherry
- 1 can cannellini beans, drained
- ¾ cup black olives
- ½ cup freshly chopped parsley
- 1 Tbs toasted pine nuts
- extra chorizo slices, to garnish

Season the chicken with salt and pepper. Heat the olive oil in a saucepan and brown the chicken in batches (skin-side down first). Remove when golden brown on both sides.

In the same saucepan, place the onions, celery, chorizo, garlic, red pepper, bay leaves and smoked paprika, and gently fry till softened.

Stir in the raisins, tomatoes, tomato purée and sherry, and bring to the boil. Turn the heat down and simmer gently with the lid on until the sauce begins to thicken.

Adjust the seasoning, return the chicken to the pot and simmer gently for 15 minutes. Add the beans and olives, and simmer for 10 minutes more. Stir in the parsley and remove from the heat.

Spoon into a large bowl, scatter with pine nuts and chorizo slices, and serve with parsley rice or earthy crushed new potatoes drizzled with olive oil.

TIP: If you can't find smoked paprika replace with ordinary paprika.

SERVES 4

Chickpea Mash with Chorizo Chunks

- 3 Tbs olive oil
- 1 cup roughly chopped, skinless chorizo sausage
- 1 red onion, finely chopped
- 1 large red pepper, roughly chopped
- 1 sliced or whole red chilli
- 4 cloves garlic, finely chopped
- 1 tsp finely chopped ginger
- 2 tsp toasted cumin seeds, bashed
- 1 long stick celery, thinly sliced
- 1 cup cherry tomatoes
- ½ cup white wine
- 2 cups cooked chickpeas
- salt and freshly ground black pepper
- large handful Italian parsley, roughly chopped
- zest of 1 very ripe lemon
- 1 Tbs butter

It seems that wherever we stopped for a tapas snack, chickpeas and chorizo would be served in some shape or form. Manolo said that if these two ingredients were in any Spanish home, nobody would ever go hungry. I made sure that I filled my suitcase with chorizo sausages to enjoy at home; you could in those days, but what my clothes smelled like is another story!

Heat the oil in a large non-stick frying pan, add the chorizo sausage and fry for three minutes. Add the onion and red pepper and cook for five minutes, stirring all the time.

Add the chilli, garlic, ginger, cumin seeds, celery and cherry tomatoes, and cook for five minutes. Add the wine and chickpeas, season with salt and pepper, and simmer for a further five minutes, adding a little liquid if it starts to stick.

Stir in the parsley, lemon zest and butter, and give the chickpeas a rough mash. Adjust the seasoning and remove from the heat.

This chickpea mash is delicious topped with sausages and served with a fresh cos and red onion salad. Dress the salad with a simple lemon vinaigrette and top with shaved Parmesan cheese.

SERVES 4

I really love the potent perfume of fresh quinces; their fragrance just fills the room. When I was young, my father used to eat ripe quinces with salt, but my mother would poach them and serve them with custard. I love the dry, astringent flavour of these fuzzy-covered fruits and I serve them as an accompaniment to roast meats (such as pork, chicken, guinea fowl, quail and game) but they also work well with cheese.

Roasted Quinces

- 6 fragrant unblemished ripe quinces
- ¼ cup sugar
- 30 g butter

Preheat the oven to 220 °C. Peel the quinces, core and quarter them. Place the quarters in a baking dish, sprinkle with the sugar and dot with butter.

Close with foil and bake till tender; about 35 minutes. Remove the foil and grill the quinces till they caramelise. Serve as an accompaniment to roasted meats, or serve as a dessert with cream, custard or vanilla ice cream.

SERVES 6

Spanish-inspired Jenny Salad

- 1 red onion, very thinly sliced
- ½ cup pitted green olives
- ½ cup chopped flat leaf parsley
- 3 Tbs sultanas
- 2 tsp lemon zest
- 1 tsp fresh thyme leaves
- ½ tsp smoked paprika
- ½ cup olive oil
- ¼ cup red wine vinegar
- 1 clove garlic, crushed
- salt and ground black pepper
- 1 cup cooked chickpeas, drained
- 200 g cos lettuce, chilled
- 1 Tbs toasted pine nuts

Place the onion slices, olives, parsley, sultanas, lemon zest, thyme, paprika, olive oil, vinegar and garlic in a bowl. Season with salt and pepper, and give it a good stir. Gently stir in the chickpeas and let the flavours mingle for an hour or so.

Just before you are ready to serve, tear the lettuce into bite-sized pieces and arrange on a serving platter. Spoon the chickpea salad over the lettuce, scatter over the pine nuts and serve.

SERVES 6

Manolo said that romesco sauce originated in Tarragona, in north-eastern Spain, where it was made by the local fishermen of the area to eat with fish. He warned that as it is like Spanish tomato sauce and can be served with so many dishes, I had better learn to make a good one to keep my husband happy!

Pork with Salsa Romesco on Crushed White Beans

SALSA ROMESCO

- ⅔ cup extra virgin olive oil
- 1 slice crustless white bread
- 3 cloves garlic, finely chopped
- 1 small red pepper, diced
- ½ tsp paprika
- 3 red chillies, deseeded
- 3 ripe tomatoes, deseeded and roughly chopped
- ½ cup toasted almonds, roughly chopped
- 2 tsp lemon zest
- 4 Tbs red wine vinegar
- 3 Tbs white balsamic vinegar
- salt and freshly ground black pepper

PORK CHOPS

- 4 × pork loin chops, 200 g each, trimmed
- salt and freshly ground black pepper
- olive oil

Make the sauce a few hours before serving it so that the flavours can develop.

Heat two tablespoons of olive oil and fry the bread till nice and golden. Break it up into the bowl of your food processor.

Add another tablespoon of oil to the pan and very gently fry the garlic, red pepper and paprika for about two minutes. Spoon the mixture onto the bread. Reserve a tablespoon of oil and then add the remaining oil, chillies, tomatoes and almonds, and process till smooth.

With the motor running, drizzle the tablespoon of oil into the tomatoes. Once it is all absorbed, add the lemon zest, and then process again while drizzling in the vinegar. Season with salt and pepper, and set aside.

Season the chops with salt and pepper. Heat the olive oil and fry the chops till golden and cooked through.

To serve, place a mound of mashed beans onto the serving plate (see page 54 for recipe), top with the chops and spoon the warmed salsa romesco alongside.

TIP: I like to serve any extra sauce garnished with a few slices of toasted bread.

SERVES 4

Although most of the world's saffron is produced in Iran, Spain is the largest exporter of this spice. Individual crocus stigmas are collected by hand and as there are only a few of them in each flower, this makes saffron the most expensive spice in the world. Luckily, a little goes a long way. These red-gold threads were highly prized by pharaohs and kings as an aphrodisiac, yet it is said that large amounts produce deathly narcotic effects, so don't think of it as nature's Viagra!

Honey Saffron Orange Duck

- 4 whole duck legs
- salt and freshly ground black pepper
- 1 Tbs olive oil
- 1 big onion, thinly sliced
- 2 cloves garlic, crushed
- 1 tsp ground cumin
- 1 cinnamon stick
- 2 tsp harissa paste (see recipe on page 92)
- ¾ tsp saffron strands
- juice of 2 oranges
- zest of 1 orange
- 1½ cups chicken stock
- ⅓ cup runny honey
- ¾ cup olives
- ½ cup chopped parsley
- 2 Tbs coriander, chopped

Season the duck legs with salt and pepper. Heat the olive oil in a large saucepan and gently brown the duck. Remove and set aside.

Add the onion, garlic, cumin, cinnamon, harissa paste and saffron to the same pan, and fry gently till aromatic. Add a little orange juice to stop it catching. Cook for five minutes.

Stir in the rest of the orange juice, zest, chicken stock and honey, bring to the boil and add the duck legs. Bring the heat down and simmer for 30 minutes. Stir in the olives and parsley, and heat through. Adjust the seasoning if necessary, stir in the coriander and remove from the heat.

Serve with the sauce spooned over the duck.

SERVES 4

Manolo took us to a really small restaurant with only a few tables and we had the most delicious oxtail stew I have ever tasted. He told us that all the restaurants next to the bullrings served their own versions of oxtail stew, but that the best one he had ever tasted was made for him by a gypsy.

Oxtail Pot

- 2.5 kg oxtail portions
- salt
- freshly ground black pepper
- flour for dusting
- 3 Tbs olive oil
- 3 medium onions, chopped
- 3 sticks celery, chopped
- 2 carrots, peeled and chopped
- 1½ tsp smoked paprika
- ½ tsp dry crushed chilli
- 1½ tsp ground cumin
- ½ tsp ground cinnamon
- 1 Tbs tomato paste
- 4 cloves garlic, crushed
- 3 cups chicken or beef stock
- ¾ cup white wine
- 150 g pre-soaked green or brown lentils
- 1 cup green olives stuffed with pimento
- ½ cup chopped flat leaf parsley

Season the oxtail with salt and pepper and then dust with flour. Heat the oil in a large heavy-based saucepan and gently brown the oxtail portions in batches. Remove from the saucepan and set aside.

In the same saucepan, add the onions, celery and carrots, and cook stirring for about six minutes over a gentle heat or until the onions are translucent. Stir in the paprika, chilli, cumin, cinnamon and tomato paste, and cook for a few minutes till fragrant.

Stir in the garlic and add the oxtail, giving it a good stir to coat with the spices. Add the stock and the wine, then turn up the heat and bring to the boil. Cover the saucepan, turn the heat down and simmer gently for about two hours. Add the lentils and cook till they soften.

Stir in the olives and chopped parsley, check the seasoning and serve immediately.

TIP: Add more stock if needed and add the lentils only when the meat is tender and starting to separate from the bone.

SERVES 4 TO 6

Our Spanish host told us that the origin of paella has been traced to the region of Valencia in south-eastern Spain, where rice is grown extensively. He said that the field workers used to make it for their lunch and would add whatever they could find, such as wild rabbit, chicken, pork, veggies and chorizo. It was a hearty and delicious dish that kept them going for the rest of the day.

There are literally hundreds of versions of paella and they can be simple or really luxurious. But in Spain it is all about the rice. It is the short-grain rice from Valencia, which is so wonderful at sucking up all the flavours added to it, that makes all the difference. The secret is never to stir it once everything is in the pan. You may have to add a little stock as you go to stop it from burning, but it is essentially a dry dish, not wet and creamy like risotto. If you don't have a paella pan, be sure to use a large flat pan so that the ingredients can cook in one layer.

Chicken and Prawn Paella

- 3 Tbs olive oil
- ½ cup chopped chorizo sausage
- 4 cloves garlic, finely chopped
- 1 large onion, chopped
- ¾ tsp paprika
- 6 skinless boneless chicken thighs, cut into bite-sized chunks
- 1 large red pepper, chopped
- 1 large green pepper, chopped
- 2 large ripe tomatoes, grated
- 500 g paella rice
- ¾ tsp saffron
- salt and ground black pepper
- 1 cup dry white wine
- 4–5 cups hot chicken stock
- 500 g deveined, prawns in their shells, trimmed of whiskers and legs
- 100 g frozen peas
- 300 g cleaned black mussels, in their shell
- ½ cup chopped fresh flat leaf parsley

Heat the olive oil in a large paella pan, add the chorizo, garlic and onion, and cook gently without burning until the onion is soft and translucent.

Add the paprika and chicken pieces to the pan and brown them all over without cooking through. Remove from the pan and set aside.

Now add the peppers and stir fry gently for two minutes. Add the tomatoes and simmer for four minutes, then stir in the rice, coating it with the tomato mix.

Stir in the saffron and season with salt and pepper. Add the wine and four cups of stock and bring to the boil. Add the chicken, turn the heat right down to low and simmer for 20 minutes.

Tuck in the prawns and cook gently for five minutes, and then scatter the peas over the top and cook for another five minutes.

Taste a grain of rice and if it is still too firm, cook for a further five minutes or so till all the liquid has been absorbed. Tuck in the mussels, cover with foil and switch off the heat. Leave it to rest for 10 minutes. Scatter with freshly chopped parsley when you serve it.

TIP: I like to tuck a few meaty mussels in their shells into the rice right at the end of cooking. It just makes it look so beautiful and tastes great too!

SERVES 6 TO 8

MOROCCO

I just love browsing in the souks of Morocco, walking through huge mounds of locally grown fruit and vegetables, beautifully fresh and bursting with flavour. The heady fragrance of ripe peaches fills the air and the aroma from a mountain of strawberries makes me wonder when last I smelled a strawberry quite like that; probably not since my childhood when we grew them ourselves.

The colours and textures are so enticing: as I walk, the recipes start whirling in my head. There are gorgeous purple brinjals; tightly-closed artichoke blossoms, which they eat stem and all so nothing goes to waste; row upon row of sundried figs; luscious velvety apricots; freshly squeezed orange juice; sticky chewy prunes. And then there are the breads and cheeses, and of course the sweets: towers of brightly coloured nougat studded with almonds and cookies dripping with honey. All you hear when you walk past is the buzzing of bees.

All these wonderful ingredients go into making food that is simple and beyond delicious. On a Moroccan table you will find lots of small plates with roasted brinjal dip, beetroot and cucumber dishes, slivered onions, pâtés, potato cakes and carrots flavoured with pepper, cumin and salt – the Moroccan trinity of spices. And gorgeous sticky sweet tomatoes and lamb shank to die for. It's amazing how with a little bit of chilli, or fresh parsley and coriander, or some preserved lemon you can make a vegetable just sit up and come to life.

I like the traditional Moroccan tagines for their slow cooking method and their versatility. I remember one made with chicken, fresh peas and artichokes – it was love at first bite. I have also tasted lamb with sticky sundried apricots, beef with prunes, and dates with preserved lemons and chicken. It's lovely simple food, from the preparation to the eating.

There's no doubt about it – Moroccan food does it for me.

I made this couscous sweet for the ladies from the couscous co-op just outside of Fez. It was a wonderful experience learning to make it from scratch with them; they were such a happy, smiling group of woman and didn't mind me tagging along. We made dough from flour and semolina, pushed it through a sieve, tossed it in flour to coat, and then finally laid the couscous out to dry.

Sweet Couscous Omelette with Date and Honey Syrup

DATE SYRUP

- 10 dates, finely chopped
- 1½ cups water
- ½ cup sugar
- 1 Tbs runny honey
- peel of 1 orange, without the pith
- 1 whole clove
- 2 tsp orange blossom water

OMELETTE

- 6 jumbo eggs
- 10 fresh mint leaves stacked, rolled and thinly sliced
- pinch of salt
- pinch of sugar
- olive oil for frying

FILLING

- 6 soft, sticky dates, chopped
- 10 soft sundried apricots, chopped
- ½ cup chopped toasted almonds
- ½ cup roughly chopped toasted walnuts
- 1 cup cream cheese
- 2 Tbs honey
- ½ tsp ground cinnamon
- zest of 1 orange
- 1 tsp orange blossom water
- 1 cup cooked couscous
- 2 Tbs toasted sesame seeds

Place all the syrup ingredients in a small saucepan and simmer till the dates are broken down; add a little more water if need be. Once the dates have cooked down and the liquid looks syrupy, remove from the heat and strain. (Reserve the date mush to stir into thick chilled yoghurt.)

To make the omelettes, whisk the eggs in a bowl and add the mint. Stir in a pinch of salt and sugar.

Heat a 20 cm frying pan till smoking hot, add 1 ml olive oil and turn the heat halfway down. Pour a tablespoon of the egg mixture into the pan and swirl to coat evenly.

As soon as the egg mixture is cooked, loosen the sides and remove from the pan with a plastic spatula. Place the omelette herb-side down on baking paper and cool. Continue making omelettes in this way until you have used up all the egg mixture.

Place all the filling ingredients, except the couscous and sesame seeds, in a mixing bowl and cream together. Stir in the couscous. Divide the mixture into 12 balls, roll them into sausages, and then press them into the sesame seeds.

Top each omelette with a couscous sausage, roll it up and place it on a serving platter. When all the omelettes have been rolled in this way, serve drizzled with the date syrup.

SERVES 6

There's a place on the coast called the Medina of Essaouira, a beautiful fortified seaport town with fairy-tale battlements the colour of honey. In the port, little blue fishing boats bob up and down on the water and the fishermen sell every kind of seafood imaginable: monster crabs and juicy prawns; the freshest eels, octopus and calamari; heaps of plump sardines; lovely langoustines; and what they call crayfish with the biggest, fattest tails. It was there that I tasted the most sublime fish tagine.

My friend Christine and I were going to the local *hamam* to have a steam bath and a massage. On our way, along a narrow little alley, we met a group of workmen on their lunch break. Sitting on their haunches, their ladders up against the wall, they were busy lighting a fire under their little tagine. Into it went sardines, salt, cumin, chopped-up preserved lemons, chilli, fresh coriander, and lots and lots of olive oil. They gathered around with freshly baked flat bread ready to mop it all up.

They were very pretty boys – smooth mocha skin, white smiles, eyes so dark and full of soul – but I was more impressed with their tagine. They invited us to join them. We'd just had lunch but Christine said, "Come on, let's just have a mouthful." Well! It was the most delicious, most honest lunch I've ever eaten.

This soup is in honour of that memorable mouthful.

Essaouira Chunky Seafood Soup

- 2 Tbs olive oil
- 1 onion, finely chopped
- 3 large ripe tomatoes, grated
- 1 × 400 g tin chopped tomatoes
- 1 Tbs tomato purée
- 1 tsp ground cumin
- ½ tsp ground ginger
- 2 bay leaves
- 1 tsp ground fennel seeds
- 3 cloves garlic, crushed
- 6 cups fresh fish stock
- 2 tsp harissa paste (see page 92)
- 2 leeks, sliced
- 500 g monkfish, cut into chunks
- 500 g firm-fleshed white fish
- 4 tubes calamari, scored and sliced
- 6 large prawns, heads on, shelled and cleaned
- 100 g shrimps
- 2 red peppers, roasted, skinned and thinly sliced
- 2 Tbs chopped fresh parsley
- 2 spring onions with tops, sliced
- zest of 1 ripe lemon
- lemon wedges, to serve

Heat the olive oil in a large pot and gently fry the onion until soft and fragrant. Add the ripe tomatoes, tinned tomatoes and tomato purée, and simmer for a few minutes.

Stir in the spices and garlic and allow the flavours to infuse for about two minutes. Ladle in the fish stock and add the harissa paste, and leave to simmer for another minute or so.

Stir in the leeks, fish, calamari, prawns and shrimps, and simmer for 10 to 15 minutes.

Just before serving, add the roasted red pepper and scatter the parsley, spring onion and lemon zest over the top. Serve with fresh, ripe lemon wedges and chunks of crusty bread.

SERVES 6

Broad Bean Soup Served with Couscous Bread

SOUP
- 200 g dried broad beans
- 2 Tbs olive oil
- 1 onion, roughly chopped
- 1 leek, sliced
- 2 potatoes, cubed
- 1½ tsp paprika
- 2 tsp ground cumin
- 2 sticks celery, chopped
- 6 cloves garlic, chopped
- 1½ litres chicken or vegetable stock
- salt and pepper, to taste
- 40 g butter
- handful fresh broad beans
- 3 spring onions with tops, chopped

GARNISH
- ¼ cucumber, diced
- ½ preserved lemon, diced
- 1 tomato, seeded and diced
- ½ red onion, finely chopped
- 3 spring onions, chopped

This is my own version of a traditional soup and it was very well received when I served it in Morocco.

Place the dried broad beans in a bowl and cover with cold water. Soak overnight to rehydrate them. The following morning, drain the beans and pop off the skins.

Heat the olive oil in a large saucepan and add the onion, leek, potatoes and dried beans. Cook stirring for six minutes. Stir in the paprika and cumin and cook for five minutes.

Add the celery, garlic and stock, cover the saucepan and simmer gently for about an hour or until the beans are soft and breaking up. Add some extra stock if you need it.

While the soup is bubbling away, melt the butter in a small pan and gently sweat the fresh broad beans and spring onions until softened. Set aside.

When the soup is ready, remove it from the stove, blend till smooth and season with salt and pepper. If the soup is too thick, thin it down with a little more liquid. Stir in the broad bean and spring onion mix to add a little texture.

Ladle the soup into bowls and sprinkle with the garnish ingredients and some chopped herbs, such as fresh dill, parsley and coriander. Serve with freshly baked flat breads.

TIP: Do not add the salt while the beans are cooking as it will cause them to toughen.

SERVES 6

Jenny's Couscous Flat Breads

- 2 cups cake flour
- 1 cup couscous (pre-soaked in enough water to cover)
- 2 tsp salt
- 4 tsp sugar
- 10 g instant yeast
- 1 Tbs olive oil
- 1½ cups lukewarm water

Place all the dry ingredients in a large bowl and make a well in the centre. Pour the oil and three-quarters of the water into the well and mix to a soft dough. Add a little more water if need be, or if the dough is too wet, add a little extra flour.

Knead the dough until it is smooth and elastic to the touch; about 15 minutes. Return the dough to the bowl, oil the top and cover with a clean cloth. Leave it in a warm place to rise to twice its size.

Preheat the oven to 180 °C. Punch the dough down and divide into 12 balls.

Roll six of the balls out into rounds the size of a side plate. Roll the other six balls into sausages long enough to create a rim around the edge of the rounds. Press the 'rims' firmly into place and transfer the flat breads to a floured baking sheet.

Leave to rise to twice the size and bake for 15 to 20 minutes until golden brown. Serve warm.

MAKES 6

Brinjal Pâté

- olive oil, for frying
- 3 large brinjals
- ½ preserved lemon, chopped
- 2 Tbs roughly chopped fresh coriander
- 2 Tbs chopped flat leaf parsley
- 1 Tbs ready-made tahini
- 2 cups natural yoghurt
- 1 clove garlic, crushed
- juice of ½ lemon
- 1 tsp roughly ground toasted cumin seeds
- freshly ground black pepper
- extra parsley, to garnish

Place the brinjals onto the open flame on a gas ring and keep turning till they soften. (I usually fire up three gas rings and cook them all at the same time.)

Place the grilled brinjals in a glass bowl and cover with plastic wrap and leave to sweat. Once they have cooled, remove the skins, slice open, scrape away the seeds and chop the flesh into small pieces.

Now mix the preserved lemon, coriander, parsley, tahini and yoghurt together, and add the garlic, lemon juice and cumin. Place in the bowl of a food processor and blend till smooth.

Place the brinjal pieces in a serving bowl and season with pepper. Stir in the herb and yoghurt mixture, sprinkle with some chopped parsley and serve.

SERVES 4 TO 6

Red Pepper Pâté

- 8 large red peppers, roasted and skinned
- 5 cloves garlic, chopped
- 200 g toasted whole almonds, chopped
- salt, to taste
- 1 cup olive oil
- 4 Tbs lemon juice
- handful fresh coriander, chopped
- handful flat leaf parsley with stems, chopped

This pâté is deliciously addictive. Serve with a platter of vegetables suitable for dipping, toasted flat bread, garlic crostini and cold meats.

Place all the ingredients in a blender and process until smooth. Taste and adjust the seasoning to your liking, and serve.

SERVES 4 TO 6

Red Onion and Orange Salad

- 2 red onions, thinly sliced and salted lightly
- 4 oranges, peeled and thinly sliced
- 1 red pepper, thinly sliced
- 1 orange, juiced and zested
- 1 Tbs chopped fresh coriander
- 2 Tbs chopped chives

Arrange the onion, orange and red pepper slices on a platter. Drizzle with the orange juice and garnish with the zest and chopped herbs. Serve immediately.

SERVES 4 TO 6

Warm Moroccan Lentil Salad

- 1 cup brown lentils, soaked overnight
- 2 Tbs olive oil
- 1 small red onion, sliced
- 1 tsp tomato paste
- 1 large tomato, deseeded and chopped
- 1 clove garlic, crushed
- 2 sticks celery, thinly sliced
- 1 tsp cumin, toasted and crushed
- salt and pepper, to taste
- 2 Tbs roughly chopped parsley
- 2 Tbs roughly chopped coriander
- some extra chopped herbs, to garnish
- 1 large tomato, deseeded, quartered and cut into petals

Rinse the lentils and cook them in unsalted water for about 15 minutes until tender, but still firm.

Heat the oil in a saucepan, gently fry the onions and tomato paste until the onions are soft. Add the chopped tomato and cook for a minute or two. Add the garlic, celery and cumin, and cook for a few minutes. Season to taste.

Gently stir in the lentils and chopped herbs, and remove from the heat. Spoon into a serving dish and garnish with some chopped herbs and the tomato petals.

SERVES 4

Minted Butter Bean and Chickpea Salad

THE DRESSING

- ⅓ cup fresh lemon juice
- ⅔ cup extra virgin olive oil
- 1 tsp dark brown sugar
- 1 clove garlic, crushed
- 2 Tbs pomegranate molasses (optional)
- salt and pepper, to taste

THE SALAD

- 3 cups cooked butter beans
- 2 cups cooked chickpeas
- ½ cup roughly chopped fresh mint
- ½ Tbs chopped fresh dill
- 3 Tbs roughly chopped fresh coriander
- 2 tsp fresh lemon zest, without the pith
- 2 cloves crushed garlic
- 1 red chilli, finely diced
- 1 small red onion, finely diced
- 3 Tbs capers
- ½ cup roughly chopped Italian parsley
- 1 cup roughly chopped spring onions with tops
- salt and freshly ground black pepper
- 4 firm ripe tomatoes, roughly chopped
- ½ cup toasted pine nuts
- 1 cup roughly chopped toasted walnuts
- 200 g feta cheese, roughly crumbled

Place all the dressing ingredients in a screw-top jar and give it a good shake. Taste and adjust the seasoning to suit your palate. Set aside.

Place all the salad ingredients, except the tomatoes, pine nuts, walnuts and feta cheese, in a large bowl. Pour over the dressing and, using your hands, gently toss everything together to coat well.

Keep in the fridge and remove 30 minutes before serving. Once again with clean hands, pull the chopped tomatoes, pine nuts, walnuts and feta through the salad, and serve immediately.

TIP: If you would like a little more dressing with the salad, make twice the amount and keep whatever you don't use for a salad of baby leaves.

SERVES 6 TO 8

Moroccan Chicken Salad

THE DRESSING
- ½ tsp ground cinnamon
- 2 tsp toasted cumin seeds, roughly ground
- 2 tsp finely chopped fresh thyme
- ½ cup chopped preserved lemon
- 2 Tbs honey
- 1 clove garlic, crushed
- 1 Tbs apple cider vinegar
- 4 Tbs extra virgin olive oil
- 2 Tbs toasted pine nuts, roughly chopped

THE CHICKEN
- 4 chicken breasts, on the bone with skin on
- 2 cloves garlic, crushed
- 2 tsp fresh thyme leaves
- 1 Tbs olive oil
- 1 tsp toasted coriander seeds
- salt and freshly ground black pepper

THE SALAD
- 50 g baby spinach
- 50 g radicchio
- 50 g rocket
- 100 g butter lettuce
- 2 Tbs chopped mint
- 4 ripe figs, quartered
- 400 g drained artichoke hearts, sliced
- ½ cup pomegranate seeds
- 50 g shaved Parmesan

I saw thyme growing wild and abundant all over Morocco where it is not only used as a popular flavouring herb, but is also sold as a medicinal herb in all the markets.

Shake the ingredients for the dressing together, taste and adjust the seasoning. Set aside.

Preheat the oven to 190 °C. Place the chicken breasts onto an oven tray. Mix the garlic, thyme, olive oil and coriander together, and rub all over the chicken breasts. Season with salt and pepper and roast till the skin is crisp and the flesh moist and tender. Remove from the oven and rest until needed.

Mix together the salad leaves and mint and pile onto a platter. Slice the chicken off the bone and arrange onto the leaves with the figs and artichokes. Dress the salad, scatter over the pomegranate seeds and shaved Parmesan cheese, and serve immediately.

SERVES 4 TO 6

While I was filming with Food Network, I was introduced to a delightful Berber family in a little village called Ait Ouzzine. They lived in complete rhythm with the seasons, eating only what had been harvested or reared on their own land or what could be caught or foraged. It was as if time had stood still: they collected wood in the mountains every day when they took the goats and sheep to graze, and they stockpiled for the winter.

While they were bundling up sticks and twigs to take home, the mother told them to look for lizards so that they could make me a very special mountain tagine. I said my prayers and they were answered, for the deeper they pushed their sticks into the holes, the deeper the lizards burrowed down.

With a happy heart, I promised to make them a fruity lamb tagine instead.

Saharan Lamb Stuffed with Couscous and Fruit

- 1.5 kg deboned leg of lamb

FLAVOURED BUTTER

- 3 cloves garlic, crushed
- 1 tsp smoked paprika
- 1 tsp ground cumin
- ½ tsp freshly ground white pepper
- ¼ tsp ground cinnamon
- ½ tsp crushed dried chillies
- ¼ tsp ground cloves
- ½ tsp ground coriander
- ¾ tsp salt
- 100 g soft butter

COUSCOUS STUFFING

- 2 tsp olive oil
- ½ cup chopped onion
- ½ cup finely chopped red pepper
- ½ cup finely chopped carrot
- handful dates, pitted and chopped
- 10 almonds, toasted and chopped
- 10 walnuts, toasted and chopped
- 2 Tbs sultanas
- 2 Tbs cranberries
- 10 prunes, pitted and chopped
- 2 dried figs chopped
- 10 dried apricots chopped
- 1 Tbs chopped preserved lemon
- ¼ tsp ground cinnamon
- ¼ tsp ground ginger
- 1 cup cooked couscous
- ½ cup chopped parsley
- salt and pepper, to taste

FOR THE CASSEROLE BASE

- 2 onions, cut into thick slices
- 1 preserved lemon, thinly sliced
- 1 garlic bulb
- some dried fruit, for scattering
- 250 ml chicken stock

Make the flavoured butter first. Place all the ingredients into a bowl, mix well and chill. Remove from the fridge 20 minutes before you need it and set aside.

Now make the couscous stuffing. Heat the olive oil in a saucepan, and sweat the onion for a minute or two. Add the remaining ingredients, except the couscous and parsley. Season the mixture with salt and pepper and stir over a moderate heat for five minutes, adding a little water if it starts to stick. Remove from the heat and stir in the couscous and parsley.

Preheat the oven to 160 °C. Lay the lamb onto a flat surface and open it up gently with a knife. Spread the flavoured butter paste onto both sides of the butterflied lamb. Spread the couscous filling onto the lamb and roll it up tightly, securing with string or toothpicks.

Scatter the casserole base ingredients, except the chicken stock, over the bottom of a casserole dish or deep oven tray. Place the stuffed lamb on top and pour over the chicken stock. Cover with foil and roast in the preheated oven for two-and-a-half hours or until cooked.

TIP: I like to use a few dried apricots, figs, prunes, dates and cranberries for scattering over the base of the casserole dish.

SERVES 6

Moroccan Tomato-poached Eggs with Sausage Nuggets

- 200 g really good-quality sausage
- 2 Tbs olive oil
- 1 small onion, chopped
- 3 cloves garlic, crushed
- 2 tsp toasted cumin seeds, roughly ground
- ½ tsp ground cinnamon
- ½ tsp ground ginger
- 1 × 400 g can chopped tomatoes
- 3 Tbs chopped fresh coriander
- 3 Tbs chopped fresh flat leaf parsley
- 4 fresh jumbo eggs
- extra chopped coriander and parsley, for scattering

Remove the sausage meat from the casing and roll into balls the size of a large green olive. Set aside until needed.

Heat the olive oil in a small saucepan and fry the onion, garlic, cumin, cinnamon and ginger gently together for three minutes, stirring.

Add the tomatoes, coriander and parsley, and cook for five minutes. Place the tomato mixture in a food processor and process till smooth.

Transfer the tomato mixture to a deep non-stick pan and heat gently. Add the sausage balls and stir to cover. Break the eggs onto the tomato sauce and cook till done the way you like them.

Garnish with chopped coriander and parsley, and serve from the pan at the table with chunks of ciabatta to mop up the sauce.

SERVES 4

While I was filming for Food Network with a Bedouin and his young family who lived in the Sahara desert, I made these stuffed peppers for them. They never got to eat a lot of meat and only had fresh fruit and vegetables when they shopped once a month in the nearest town. I thought that this dish had everything they would enjoy and looked forward to treating them.

Once the dish was assembled I was about to pack the peppers into the pan to go in the fire but was stopped by the children. They wanted to eat them just like that, relishing the crisp crunch of the fresh peppers. Thank goodness the filling was cooked!

Saharan Stuffed Peppers

- 4 cloves garlic, crushed
- 1 Tbs chopped fresh ginger
- salt, to taste
- 1 onion, finely chopped
- 1 carrot, finely chopped
- zest of 1 lemon
- ½ cup sultanas
- ½ cup dried apricots, chopped
- 4 whole cardamom pods, split
- 1 tsp paprika
- 1 tsp cinnamon
- 1 tsp dried chilli
- 1 tsp cumin
- 1 tsp turmeric
- 2 tomatoes, roughly chopped
- handful parsley, chopped
- handful coriander, chopped
- 1 stalk soup celery, finely chopped
- 250 g finely chopped lamb
- 1 Tbs olive oil
- 1 cup cooked rice
- 2 red peppers
- 2 yellow peppers
- 2 green peppers

Preheat the oven to 180 °C.

Pound the garlic and ginger in a pestle and mortar with the salt until smooth. Mix the paste with the remaining ingredients, except the rice and peppers, stirring well.

Place the mixture into a saucepan, cover tightly with foil and let it simmer for 30 minutes. Stir the lamb mixture into the rice and adjust the seasoning.

Slice the top off each pepper so that it can be used as a 'lid', and remove the seeds and pith. Spoon the lamb stuffing into each pepper and place the lid on top.

Arrange the peppers in a lightly oiled oven-proof dish and bake for 35 to 40 minutes until cooked through. Serve with a large fresh salad.

SERVES 6

While I was filming with a semi-nomadic Berber-speaking family in a little village called Ait Ouzzine, they invited me to have a picnic with them in the mountains. The two 4 × 4s were jam-packed with people, carpets, gas stoves, almonds, teapots and glasses, and the ingredients to make bourfan bread.

When we reached our picnic spot, the beautiful handmade carpets were laid out onto the barren stony ground and a large kettle went onto the little gas ring to boil. We all scurried about hunting for anything that would burn and collecting lots of little rocks and stones on which to bake the bread.

Once the makings of our 'oven' were in place, all but three of the nine sisters gathered with the two brothers and many grandchildren on the carpets to sip tea and eat almonds and tell stories.

The three sisters took charge of baking the beautiful big stuffed bread: Aicha arranged the kindling and rocks and was in charge of making and maintaining the fire; Miriam and her Aunty Cloho took turns in kneading the huge mound of dough; and Fatima pounded an aromatic paste made of herbs and spices and roasted onions that were left to dry out in the sun. Once the dough was rested, it was pressed out into a circle and the delicious spicy green paste was spread all over it, almost to the edges.

The bread was placed onto the hot stones, covered with cardboard and then sand was thrown on top of that. It was left to bake for about 45 minutes, the aroma indicating when it was time to take it out of the fire. The bread was removed and dusted till not a grain of sand remained.

The moment had come for the bread to be broken, and it is a moment I will never forget. The aroma that escaped from that steaming loaf of bread was like nothing I will ever experience again. Pure heaven! My version is for sweet little Miriam.

Bourfan Bread

THE AROMATIC PASTE

- 2 Tbs olive oil
- 1 large onion, finely chopped
- 1 cup packed with fresh coriander
- 2 dried chillies, soaked in warm water
- 3 cloves garlic, chopped
- 1 Tbs toasted cumin seeds
- 1 tsp salt
- 4 spring onions, with the green tops, chopped
- 100 g beef fat, finely chopped, or ½ cup olive oil

THE DOUGH

- 4 cups cake flour
- 2 tsp salt
- 4 tsp sugar
- 10 g instant yeast
- 1 Tbs olive oil
- 400 ml lukewarm water

First make the paste. Heat the olive oil in a large frying pan and cook the onions till they are nice and golden. Transfer the onions to a blender and add all of the remaining ingredients. Blend to a paste and set aside till needed.

Preheat the oven to 200 °C. To make the dough, place all the dry ingredients into a large mixing bowl and make a well in the centre. Add the oil and three-quarters of the water and mix to a soft dough. Add a little more water if need be, or if it is too wet add a small amount of flour.

Knead the dough until it is smooth and elastic to the touch, about 15 minutes. Return the dough to the bowl and oil the top. Cover with a clean cloth and place it in a warm place to rise to twice its size.

Press the dough out into a 38 cm circle and then spread the delicious spicy green paste all over it, almost to the edges. Bring the edges up to the centre and press tightly together – it looks like a big dumpling.

Dust the top with a little flour and bake for 30 to 40 minutes or until nice and brown and hollow-sounding when tapped. Remove from the oven and rest it for about 30 minutes before cutting.

MAKES 1 LARGE LOAF

While I was filming in Morocco I had to cook a meal for a family that owned a date plantation. I wanted to incorporate dates into a dish that was familiar to them, and so came up with my own version of a traditional favourite. They lapped up every last morsel!

Beef Kefta wrapped in Brinjal

BEEF KEFTA
- 600 g beef mince
- 2 cloves garlic, crushed
- 1 small onion, finely chopped
- 1 tsp paprika
- ¼ tsp ground nutmeg
- ¼ tsp freshly ground fennel seed
- 1 tsp ground cumin
- ½ tsp ground cinnamon
- ½ tsp chilli powder, or to taste
- salt and pepper, to taste
- 2 Tbs freshly chopped coriander
- 2 Tbs finely chopped fresh flat leaf parsley

BRINJAL WRAPS
- 4 long brinjals, thinly sliced
- salt
- olive oil

SWEET SAUCE
- 10 ml olive oil
- 1 onion, chopped
- 4 cloves garlic, crushed
- 1 red pepper, diced
- 1 × 400 g tin chopped tomatoes
- 1 × 400 g tin whole peeled tomatoes
- 1 tsp cumin
- 1 tsp fennel
- dried chilli, crushed, to taste
- 1 cup dates, pitted and chopped
- salt and pepper, to taste

Mix all the kefta ingredients together, pinch off large walnut-sized pieces and roll into bullet-shaped sausages. Heat a little oil in a non-stick pan and brown the kefta on all sides, and then allow to cool. They don't need to be fully cooked, as they will cook further in the tomato sauce.

Salt the brinjal slices and allow to drain for 15 to 20 minutes, then rinse and pat dry. Fry the brinjal slices on one side until softened. Set aside.

To make the sauce, heat the olive oil in a wide saucepan and sauté the onion till soft and fragrant. Add the garlic and red pepper and stir for a few more seconds.

Add the tinned tomatoes, spices and dates, and allow the sauce to simmer gently.

Wrap a slice of brinjal around each beef kefta and place the rolls in the sauce. Allow to simmer for 15 minutes.

Serve on a bed of couscous, scattered with extra chopped parsley.

SERVES 4

Quick Moroccan Spice Mix

I like to dry-roast my cardamom, cumin, allspice seeds and black pepper and then grind them separately. Store the mix in the freezer if you have any left over.

- ½ tsp ground cloves
- ½ tsp cayenne pepper
- 2 tsp ground cumin
- 2 tsp ground ginger
- 2 tsp turmeric
- 2 tsp allspice
- 2 tsp cardamom
- 2 tsp black pepper
- 3 tsp coriander seeds
- 3 tsp ground cinnamon
- 3 tsp ground nutmeg

Mix it all together and seal in an airtight container. I like to use this spice mix for adding to meatballs, tagines and rubbing onto roasts.

MAKES 1 SMALL JAR

By roasting spices, their wonderful volatile oils are released and this intensifies their flavour. Spices lose their fragrance and flavour quickly, so don't make more than you need at any one time.

Easy Harissa

This fiery paste differs from one household to the next. It is very easy to make and store, and is excellent for stews, tagines, stir fries and rubbing onto roasts.

- 100 g dried chillies
- 12 cloves garlic
- ⅓ cup salt
- ½ cup coriander seeds, toasted and ground
- ⅓ cup cumin seeds, toasted and ground
- 2 tsp toasted caraway seeds
- 1 tsp ground cinnamon
- 1 Tbs dried mint
- ½ bunch fresh coriander
- ⅔ cup olive oil

Soften the chillies in a little hot water and drain. Place all the ingredients, except the olive oil, in a food processor. With the motor running, make a paste by slowly adding the olive oil.

Transfer the paste to a frying pan and cook stirring for a minute. Bottle and when the paste cools store it in the fridge. Be sure to keep it topped with olive oil so that it does not dry out.

TIP: I always use the whole seeds of cumin and coriander, toasted first and then ground for maximum flavour.

MAKES ABOUT 1 ½ CUPS

I was filming in the weekly market in Azrou and as I wanted something quick and tasty that could be cooked over the fire, I decided on kebabs. Just as I was pouring honey onto the kebabs, I heard a man say, "I followed this delicious aroma all over the market till I found it." He offered me two juicy oranges in exchange for a taste of what I was cooking.

I cry every time I tell the story – this poor old man was blind and he said that he would forever lock that delicious aroma away in his heart and mind.

Azrou Kebabs

- 1.5 kg lamb or chicken breast fillets, skinned and deboned, cut into thin slices
- 1 level tsp ground ginger
- 4 cloves garlic, crushed
- 1 level tsp paprika
- 1 heaped tsp cumin seeds, toasted and roughly bashed
- ½ tsp ground cinnamon
- handful fresh parsley, chopped
- handful fresh mint, chopped
- handful fresh coriander, chopped
- salt, to taste
- freshly ground black pepper
- runny honey, for brushing

Place the meat into a glass bowl, add the spices and chopped fresh herbs, and toss well so that the chunks are completely coated. Marinate for 30 minutes.

While the meat is marinating, soak some wooden skewers in cold water for about 20 minutes – then the wood won't burn when you grill your kebabs.

Thread the meat onto the skewers and season with salt and pepper. Grill under a hot grill or over an open fire till done. Brush with some honey just before serving, and seal on the heat for a few seconds.

Serve with sultana couscous and red onions and minted yoghurt, or lemon sautéed potatoes and a large green salad.

TIP: If you add any type of acid, such as lemon juice or wine, to your marinade when using chicken breasts do not leave them longer than an hour – the flesh will break down and become mealy.

SERVES 6 TO 8

This is a meal with a difference because the Moroccan housewife prepares it as she shops.

Using a traditional tangia, which is an urn-shaped clay cooking vessel, she goes around the market adding her bits and pieces to the pot. Her last stop is at the butcher where she buys some meat. He usually adds his own spice blend to the tangia and seals it for her. She then takes it to be cooked at a female *hamam* – which is a traditional Moroccan bathhouse – where the coals that heat the water for the baths also cook the food.

Hours later the housewife returns to collect her tangia, her dinner soft and fragrant, and ready to be served to her family.

While I was in Morocco I got to cook my own tangia at the local *hamam* and that is where I met Mohammed. He had been stoking the fire for the *hamam* for over two decades and, to earn a little more on the side, he slow-cooked tangias for the local community. He would take those beautiful hot glowing ashes from the fire and would bury the pots in them, leaving the food to simmer away slowly for hours. This is the slowest, most flavoursome cooking you're ever going to get.

Beef and Prune Tangia

- 1 large onion, finely chopped
- 1.5 kg beef shin
- 1 cup roughly chopped prunes
- 2 tomatoes, chopped
- 2 Tbs honey
- salt and pepper, to taste
- 2 cloves garlic, chopped
- 2 Tbs Quick Moroccan Spice Mix, see page 92
- 2 Tbs olive oil
- 3 Tbs chopped flat leaf parsley
- 3 Tbs chopped fresh coriander
- 1 small preserved lemon, chopped
- 1 chilli, chopped
- 1½ cups chicken stock

Preheat the oven to 170 °C. Place all the ingredients, except the chicken stock, into a large bowl and mix together well to coat.

Place the meat into a tangia (an oven-proof dish or tagine will work just as well), pour the chicken stock around the meat, cover tightly and bake in the oven for two hours. Check the meat for tenderness and if it needs more time, leave it in the oven for a little longer.

Serve with freshly baked rounds of Moroccan bread or some couscous.

TIP: This tangia can also be cooked in a heavy-bottomed saucepan on the stove. Take care to cover it tightly.

SERVES 4 TO 6

Have you ever been surrounded by that sweet perfume of more quinces than you have ever seen in your life, all heaped together, just waiting for a tagine? The wonderful thing about the quince is that once the heat gets to it and you leave a bit of the skin in the pot, it brings out this delicate pink blush on the dense, astringent, white flesh. My father taught me to eat fresh quinces with salt – dry and yummy.

Saffron Lamb

- 2 Tbs olive oil
- 4 lamb shanks
- salt and pepper, to taste
- 1 large onion, chopped
- 4 saffron strands
- 2 tsp ground cumin
- ½ tsp ground ginger
- ½ tsp ground cardamom
- ½ tsp ground cinnamon
- 3 cloves garlic, chopped
- 1 Tbs tomato paste
- 1 × 400 g can chopped tomatoes
- 5 tomatoes grated
- 12 plump prunes, pitted
- 1 cinnamon stick
- 2 to 3 quinces, peeled and quartered
- 1 Tbs runny honey
- 2 Tbs chopped parsley
- 2 Tbs chopped fresh coriander
- grated zest of 1 orange

Heat the oil in in a large saucepan or tagine. Season the lamb shanks with salt and pepper, and brown on all sides. Set aside.

In the same saucepan, place the onion, saffron, cumin, ginger, cardamom, ground cinnamon and garlic, and cook gently till the spices become aromatic.

Add the tomato paste and cook for a few seconds. Then add the tinned chopped tomatoes, fresh tomatoes, prunes, cinnamon stick and quinces, and bring to the boil. Add the lamb shanks and honey, turn the heat down and simmer gently for an hour.

Stir in the herbs and orange zest, remove from the heat and serve with freshly baked bread.

TIP: Add a little chicken stock if the tagine looks dry.

SERVES 4

As the sun goes down, the Djemaa El Fna square in Marrakech transforms into a Mecca of vibrant food stands, teaming with hungry customers. You are bound to find whatever you are looking for on one of the hundreds of stalls there – anything from snails to sheep's heads! I got to cook for the locals on stall 117; it was a gas cooking for the hungry happy stallholders.

Moroccan Fry-up of Chicken, Olives and Preserved Lemon

- 2 Tbs olive oil
- 8 skinned, deboned chicken thighs, cut into bite-sized pieces
- a good shake of white pepper
- 3 cm fresh ginger, finely chopped
- 4 cloves garlic, finely chopped
- 8 spring onions with tops, roughly chopped
- 1 preserved lemon, finely chopped
- 1 cup halved pitted green olives
- 1 Tbs butter
- 2 Tbs chopped fresh coriander
- 2 Tbs chopped flat leaf parsley

Heat the oil in a large frying pan, and add the chicken, white pepper, ginger and garlic. Cook stirring on a high heat for five minutes.

Now stir in the spring onions and preserved lemon and cook for a further five minutes. Stir in the olives and butter and cook for five minutes more.

Stir in the fresh herbs and serve immediately with couscous or boiled herbed potatoes.

SERVES 4

Mohammed's Mint Tea

As the Moroccans drink their tea extremely sweet, I prefer to start with just a little sugar and then my guests can add more if they like.

- 1 Tbs green tea leaves
- large handful well-washed fresh mint leaves
- 4 cups boiling water
- ¼ to ½ cup white sugar

Rinse your teapot with some boiling water, and then place the tea leaves, washed mint and sugar into the pot. Pour over the boiling water and let the tea steep for five to eight minutes before serving so that all that wonderful minty flavour is extracted from the leaves. Give the tea a stir and then serve.

Tamatert is a little village perched on the side of the High Atlas mountains over two thousand metres above sea level. It was there that I stayed in a small guesthouse owned by a Frenchwoman. After the death of her son, Jacqueline Brandt came to this remote little village, fell in love with the place and ended up turning a derelict traditional Berber home into a guesthouse that she now runs with the help of a local woman, Rashida.

While I was there, I was invited to the kitchen of a neighbour called Malika to see how she started her culinary day. I was so excited; I can't even begin to tell you how privileged I felt to be in Malika's kitchen where she made bread for her family every single day of her life.

All she did to make her beautiful, simple bread was to mix flour and water together, working it and working it until she got a really smooth and elastic dough. She added a little oil to keep it nice and moist, and then folded it over so that the oil made a separation between the layers; she did this a few times. Then she flattened it out and popped it into the pan. There was no recipe, nothing from a book, just a simple ritual that had been handed down from mother to daughter.

There was no way her husband Mohammed was going to be left out. He shared a traditional Moroccan tea ceremony with me. Making tea is a man's job, he told me.

One very special Moroccan memory I will always cherish is when I got to cook for the village elder, his wife and his gorgeous little granddaughter. The grandma didn't smile much but that all changed when she started to scoop my rice pudding into her little rosebud mouth. When she gave me a smile that almost stopped my heart, I knew she liked it.

I went to a lot of trouble to make a very special pudding for them, and even went to harvest my own honey for the dish. Well actually, I had no option as there was none to buy in the little shops. The locals all went to the hives to buy their honey directly from the beekeeper.

Hassan the beekeeper kept his hives just a short drive away from Tamatert, further up the mountains. The whole mountainside was covered in thyme, and as I walked I crushed it beneath my feet, releasing its beautiful aroma. I felt dizzy with happiness as the scent enveloped my body.

Hassan started to smoke the hives with a mixture of juniper berry, dung and thyme. He said it would confuse the bees and get them to leave the hive. I was petrified to be surrounded by all those angry bees but I really wanted the honey.

The beekeeper made me wear protective gear to prevent me from getting stung by the honey bees, but what did Crazy Woman do? She wore sandals and socks and got stung all over her feet. Oh, the pain! But that glorious thyme-flavoured honey was worth it all.

Moroccan Rice Pudding Topped with Honeyed Almonds

RICE PUDDING

- ¾ cup uncooked rice
- 3 cups milk
- 2 cups ideal milk
- 1 vanilla pod or 1 tsp vanilla extract
- 1 cinnamon stick
- 1 cup pouring cream
- ½ cup sugar
- 2 tsp cornflour, mixed to a paste with a little cold water
- 2 egg yolks, beaten
- 1–2 Tbs honey
- zest of 1 large ripe orange
- 2 tsp orange blossom water

HONEYED ALMONDS

- ½ cup runny honey
- ¾ cup whole almonds, with skin on

Place the rice in a large saucepan with all the milk, the vanilla pod and cinnamon stick. Bring to the boil and cook until the rice is tender; about 20 minutes.

Reduce the heat to moderate, add the cream and sugar, and mix well. Add the cornflour paste and stir until the mixture thickens.

Add a little of the rice to the egg yolks and stir well. Gradually pour the egg yolk mixture into the rice and continue to cook over moderate heat until creamy, stirring all the time.

Stir in the honey, orange zest and orange blossom water, and remove from the stove.

Place the honey and almonds in a small saucepan and heat gently. When the honey starts to foam, stir and cook for a minute. Remove from the heat and spoon a few honeyed almonds over each serving of rice pudding.

SERVES 4 TO 6

GREECE

Some of my happiest food memories were made in Greece. Once we stayed on the little island of Aegina, which is only about 27 km from Athens on the hydrofoil. Our little guesthouse had its own grapevine and olive trees, and a beautiful little outdoor dining area with rickety wooden chairs and a wobbly wooden table covered with a well-worn cloth.

One evening our landlady, her husband and a few friends were gathered around the table playing backgammon (the Greeks call it *tavli*) ready to tuck into a simple meal. There was a plate of crispy glistening deep-pink watermelon wedges; a bowl of ripe sweet figs; snow-white slabs of feta cheese drizzled with olive oil; bowls of large roasted pistachios; long black slightly bitter olives with pointy tips; a jug of fragrant olive oil to accompany a loaf of crusty bread that had come out of the wood oven an hour earlier, and a jug of local wine. It was a feast fit for a king, her husband said. Just thinking back on that beautiful rustic sight brings a smile to my heart.

One Sunday evening, in a little Greek town outside of Athens, the locals came out to dine at a pop-up restaurant in the park. Wooden trestles covered with white paper were set with bowls of chunky Greek salad, juicy glistening lemon wedges, freshly baked bread, swollen black olives and little jugs of green peppery olive oil.

There were fires going in half oil drums and when the coals were hot and white, huge steaks of swordfish went onto the grill. They came drizzled with olive oil and scattered with a little chilli and freshly chopped parsley.

We dined to the sound of the *bouzouki*, and drank revolting cheap wine that tasted like heaven because of the wonderful atmosphere. After much eating and dancing, the dessert was served: honey-drenched cookies, nutty pastries, Greek milk tart and sweet, aromatic Greek coffee.

We went to bed full and happy that night.

Elsa the Greek mama told me that Papoutsakia means 'little shoes' in Greek and that this homely dish is a once-weekly family standby. She said that the Greeks have hundreds of ways to cook up brinjals and that this is just one of them. According to Elsa, the Greeks gave the Indians coriander, and they gave the Greeks brinjals in exchange.

Little Shoes – *Papoutsakia*

BRINJALS

- 6 small to medium-sized brinjals
- 6 Tbs olive oil
- 1 medium onion, finely chopped
- 2 cloves garlic, crushed
- 400 g beef or lamb mince
- 5 ripe medium-sized tomatoes, very finely chopped
- 1 tsp dried oregano
- ½ cup chopped flat leaf parsley, with stems
- salt, to taste
- freshly ground black pepper
- béchamel sauce
- 1 cup grated pecorino or Parmesan
- 12 cherry tomatoes

BÉCHAMEL SAUCE

- 2 Tbs butter
- 2 Tbs flour
- 1½ cups warmed milk
- salt, to taste
- pepper, to taste
- grated nutmeg, to taste
- 2 egg yolks, beaten

Wash and dry the brinjals, trim off the stems, and cut them in half lengthwise. Using a small knife or spoon, scoop out the pulp, leaving a little intact around the shell of each brinjal so that it does not collapse. Do not to break through the skin. Chop the pulp into small pieces and set aside.

Heat two tablespoons of the oil in a saucepan and fry the onion, then add the garlic and mince and cook gently for five minutes. Stir in the brinjal pulp, tomatoes, oregano, parsley, salt and pepper, and simmer till most of the liquid from the tomatoes has been absorbed.

Remove from the heat, and set aside while you make the béchamel sauce.

Melt the butter in a saucepan over low heat and, as soon as it starts to foam, add the flour and stir with a wooden spoon until it is lump free. Remove from the heat and add the milk slowly, stirring constantly.

Return to the stove and cook until the sauce begins to thicken. Remove from the heat and season to taste with salt, pepper and nutmeg. Allow the sauce to cool for a few minutes before stirring in the egg yolks in a steady stream.

Preheat the oven to 180 °C. Heat a little oil in a frying pan and lightly sauté the top of the brinjal halves – do this in batches. Oil the base of a large roasting pan and place the brinjal halves onto it, cut-side facing up.

Spoon a little of the filling into each brinjal half, sprinkle with some of the grated cheese, and then continue spooning the filling to the top. Press down and spoon over some béchamel sauce. Garnish with a cherry tomato and a dusting of grated Parmesan.

Place in the oven and bake for about 50 minutes, or until the brinjals are tender and the tops golden brown.

SERVES 6

Grilled Swordfish

THE FISH
- 1 thick firm white fish, even tuna will do, weighing 1 kg
- butter, for dotting
- chopped parsley, to garnish

THE MARINADE
- ¾ tsp dried oregano
- 1 Tbs chopped fresh thyme leaves
- ½ tsp dried chilli flakes
- juice of 2 lemons
- zest of 1 lemon
- ½ cup olive oil
- 2 cloves garlic, finely chopped
- salt and ground black pepper

This dish conjures up memories of a wonderful evening spent dining under a starry sky to the sound of the bouzouki. Juicy swordfish steaks were served straight from the fire. Swordfish is now on SASSI's orange list, so it is preferable to use tuna or any other firm-fleshed fish when preparing this dish.

Cut the fish into four steaks and place in a shallow dish. Whisk the marinade ingredients together and pour over the fish. Marinate in the fridge for 20 minutes, turning once. If you like, you could reserve the marinade to make into a sauce. I do!

Heat a lightly oiled grilling pan until it is smoking hot. Pan-grill the fish steaks until they are almost done.

Place each steak on a plate, dot with butter and scatter with chopped parsley. Serve with a chunky salad and lemon wedges.

If you would like a little sauce to serve on the side, heat up the reserved marinade in a small saucepan while the fish is cooking. When it comes to the boil, remove it from the heat and whisk in little knobs of butter until it tastes the way you like it.

TIP: Don't overcook the fish, as it's always better when it is succulent and moist. Remember that it continues to 'cook' after it has been removed from the heat source.

SERVES 4

Gorgeous Greek Mountain Lamb

THE RUB
- 1 clove garlic, crushed
- 2 Tbs olive oil
- 1 Tbs toasted fennel seeds, ground
- 1 Tbs lemon zest
- 1 Tbs finely chopped fresh rosemary
- salt
- freshly ground black pepper
- 1 Tbs ground toasted cumin seeds

MEDITERRANEAN PASTE
- ½ cup chopped feta cheese
- ½ cup chopped black olives
- ¾ cup finely chopped sundried tomatoes
- 2 tsp dried oregano
- 2 cloves garlic, crushed
- juice of 1 ripe lemon

THE LAMB
- 1 deboned leg of lamb, about 2 kg
- olive oil, for frying
- 3 large onions, sliced into thick rings
- fresh rosemary stems
- 3 fresh bay leaves

Preheat the oven to 210 °C. Mix the rub ingredients together, and set aside. Do the same with the Mediterranean paste ingredients.

Open up the lamb and rub it inside and out with the rub mix. Now spread the paste mixture onto the inside of the meat and roll it up, tying with string or securing with toothpicks.

Heat a little olive oil in a large frying pan and brown the lamb all over. Now place a bed of sliced onions down onto the base of a roasting tray, scatter with the rosemary stems and bay leaves, and then place the lamb on top.

Cover the tray with foil, shiny side in, and place in the preheated oven. Roast for five minutes and then turn the heat right down to 150 °C. Roast slowly for two-and-a-half to three hours, or until the meat is meltingly soft.

Serve with Lentil and Spinach Rice (see page 109) or crisp and sticky roast potatoes, and a huge Greek salad.

TIP: Rest for 20 minutes before carving so that all the delicious juices go back into the meat!

SERVES 6

Lamb is a favourite meat amongst the Greeks and is eaten at all celebrations, especially during Easter. They know how to cook it long and slow so that it just melts off the bone.

We had a delicious meal in Glyfada on the quayside of a little harbour. We sipped chilled wine while we waited for our lunch order to be taken and watched the yachts bobbing up and down on the gentle ripples of the water. When we asked the waiter what he would recommend, he told us we had to have the baby calamari, deep fried white bait and *yiouvetsi*. "What is *yiouvetsi*?" I asked. He described a dish of big fat juicy prawns with feta and tomato sauce, baked till just done. He said that we had to try it. Now this is not a combination that I would necessarily choose – seafood and cheese – but the way he described it made my mouth water, so we ordered it. I am so glad we did.

Prawns with Feta and Tomatoes – *Garithes Yiouvetsi*

- 24 fat juicy prawns
- 6 Tbs olive oil
- 1 onion, chopped
- ½ red pepper, diced
- ½ yellow pepper, diced
- 700 g ripe tomatoes, roughly chopped
- ¾ tsp dried oregano
- 2 sticks celery, finely chopped
- 4 cloves garlic, chopped
- 1 chilli, chopped
- ½ cup white wine
- salt and pepper, to taste
- 2 Tbs parsley, chopped
- 1 Tbs dill
- 100 g feta, crushed
- 12 black olives

Devein the prawns and trim the feelers, but keep the heads and shells on.

Heat the olive oil in a saucepan and fry the onion and peppers until the onions are translucent. Add the tomatoes, oregano, celery, garlic, chilli and white wine, and cook until the tomatoes are reduced and thick. Season to taste.

Preheat the oven to 180 °C. Spoon the sauce into an ovenproof dish suitable for serving, stir in the herbs and tuck in the prawns. Dot with feta and olives, and bake for 25 to 30 minutes. Remove from the oven and rest for a few minutes before serving.

Serve with a mixed salad and chunks of freshly baked bread. Messy and delicious!

SERVES 4 TO 6

Potato, Bean and Tomato Sauce

- ⅓ cup olive oil
- 1 large onion, thinly sliced
- 4 large potatoes, peeled and cubed
- 2 cloves garlic, crushed
- 1 small chilli, chopped
- salt and pepper, to taste
- 500 g fresh tomatoes, grated
- 1 kg green beans, topped and tailed, roughly chopped and blanched
- ¾ cup chicken stock
- ½ cup roughly chopped parsley
- 100 g feta cheese, crumbled

This makes a delicious side dish for fish, chicken, lamb, beef and pork.

Heat the olive oil in a saucepan and add the onion, potatoes, garlic and chilli, and cook gently, stirring for five minutes. Season with salt and pepper and stir in the tomatoes.

Simmer gently till the potatoes are half cooked, and then add the beans and the chicken stock. Cook until the potatoes and beans are tender.

Stir in the parsley, pile onto a serving platter and top with the feta cheese.

SERVES 6

Lentil and Spinach Rice with Pine Nuts

- 5 Tbs olive oil
- 1 large onion, chopped
- 2 cloves garlic, crushed
- 800 g spinach, washed and chopped
- 1 cup cooked lentils
- 2 cups cooked rice
- juice of 1 lemon
- zest of 1 lemon
- salt and pepper
- 2 Tbs chopped parsley
- 3 Tbs chopped dill
- 3 Tbs pine nuts, toasted

Heat the olive oil in a large frying pan and fry the onion till it wilts. Add the garlic and when it becomes fragrant stir in the spinach.

Cook stirring for two minutes, then add the lentils, rice, lemon juice and zest, and season well with salt and pepper. Once it is warmed through, stir in the herbs and pine nuts.

Serve with wedges of lemon, olive oil and a salad of cherry tomatoes and oregano.

TIP: Serve with fish or lamb chops, or as a great vegetarian meal.

SERVES 4 TO 6

I ate this often in Greece – and I still do – with a splash of fresh lemon juice and extra olive oil, a slice of deep-fried haloumi cheese and a large Greek salad. It makes a great light meal and my vegetarian friends just love it!

Filled Cabbage Rolls with Egg and Lemon Sauce

THE CABBAGE ROLLS
- 12 large cabbage leaves
- 1 Tbs olive oil
- 1 onion, finely chopped
- 3 cloves garlic, crushed
- 600 g lean minced beef or lamb
- 1 tsp dried oregano
- ½ tsp ground cinnamon
- salt
- ¼ tsp ground white pepper
- 900 g ripe tomatoes, grated
- 1 Tbs tomato purée
- ½ cup uncooked rice
- 1 Tbs chopped mint
- 1 Tbs chopped dill
- ½ cup fresh breadcrumbs
- ½ cup white wine
- 2 ½ cups chicken stock
- ½ cup freshly squeezed lemon juice
- 1 Tbs butter

THE SAUCE
- 1 Tbs cornflour
- 2 Tbs cold water
- 2 eggs, beaten
- juice of 1 lemon
- reduced stock (from the cabbage rolls)
- salt and pepper
- 2 tsp butter

When Elsa the Greek mama first made these for me she used pork mince; you can too, if you like.

Put a large saucepan of salted water on to boil. Blanch the cabbage leaves for about five minutes; they must be pliable enough to stuff and roll. Cool the leaves and trim away any thin stems or core cutting into the leaves.

Now start on the filling. Heat the oil in a saucepan and add the onion, garlic, mince, oregano and cinnamon, and stir till it starts to brown. Season with salt and pepper.

Add the tomatoes, tomato purée and rice. Simmer for 10 minutes. Stir in the herbs and breadcrumbs and remove from the heat. Cool slightly.

Lay the leaves out onto a flat surface and place a heaped tablespoon of the mince mix into the centre of each leaf. Now fold in the sides and roll up nice and tight to keep the filling intact.

Place a large cabbage leaf on the bottom of a heavy-based saucepan large enough to hold the rolls. Pack them in and pour in the wine, stock and lemon juice. Dot with butter and season lightly. Place a heat-proof plate over the rolls to keep them from floating around and unravelling, close the lid and simmer gently for an hour.

Remove the rolls to a heat-proof dish and keep warm. Reduce the cooking liquid to a third and put it aside for the sauce.

To make the sauce, mix the cornflour and water together, stir it into the beaten eggs and add the lemon juice. Whisk in half of the hot stock, transfer to a small saucepan, add the remaining stock and simmer gently for three minutes.

Remove from the heat, season to taste and stir in the butter. Pour over the cabbage rolls and serve with a salad and steamed rice or some crusty bread.

SERVES 6

We had two wonderful dinners in a little guesthouse on the island of Aegina. I fell in love with my landlady's pastitsio; it was meaty and cheesy and very comforting, and it reminded me of the one Daphne Papadopoulos used to make when I was a young girl.

Pastitsio

- 500 g macaroni, or hollow pasta of your choice, cooked

MEAT SAUCE
- 2 Tbs olive oil
- 2 onions, diced
- 2 stalks celery, thinly sliced
- 4 cloves garlic, finely chopped
- 1 kg lean lamb or beef mince
- 1 tsp dried oregano
- ¾ tsp ground cinnamon
- ¼ tsp ground or freshly grated nutmeg
- 1 × 400 g can tomatoes
- 3 large ripe fresh tomatoes, finely chopped
- 1 Tbs tomato paste
- ¾ cup dry red wine
- salt and freshly ground black pepper
- 1 tsp chopped fresh rosemary
- ½ cup freshly chopped parsley

CHEESE SAUCE
- 2 Tbs butter
- 2 Tbs flour
- 1½ cups warmed milk
- ¾ cup grated mature cheddar cheese
- salt, to taste
- pepper, to taste
- grated nutmeg, to taste
- 2 egg yolks, beaten
- ½ cup grated Parmesan, for sprinkling

To make the meat sauce, heat the oil in a saucepan and add the onions and celery. Cook till the onions have reduced to half their original size, and then add the garlic and mince and cook for five minutes.

Stir in oregano, cinnamon and nutmeg, and cook for another five minutes. Add the tomatoes, tomato paste, wine, salt and pepper, and simmer for 60 minutes or until the sauce thickens. Stir in the rosemary and parsley, and set aside.

To make the cheese sauce, melt the butter in a saucepan over low heat and, as soon as it starts to foam, add the flour and stir with a wooden spoon until it is lump free. Remove from the heat and add the milk slowly, stirring constantly.

Return to the stove and cook until the sauce begins to thicken. Stir in the cheddar cheese. Remove from the heat and season to taste with salt, pepper and nutmeg. Allow the sauce to cool for a few minutes before stirring in the egg yolks in a steady stream.

Let's put the dish together. Preheat the oven to 180 °C and lightly butter a 24 cm × 28 cm oven-proof dish.

Now mix one cup of cheese sauce with the cooked pasta. Spoon half of the pasta onto the base of your buttered dish and then spread half of the meat sauce onto that. Spoon a cup of cheese sauce onto that and sprinkle with half the grated Parmesan. Spoon over the rest of the pasta and then top with the remaining meat sauce. Spread the last cup of cheese sauce onto that and sprinkle the last of the grated Parmesan over the top.

Bake for about 45 to 50 minutes, or until the top is a gorgeous golden brown, and remove from the oven.

Let the pastitsio rest for at least 10 minutes before you cut it into blocks. Serve with a salad of cucumber, olives, chunks of tomato, red onion, green pepper, feta and parsley, all dressed with a lemon vinaigrette and a sprinkle of dried oregano.

SERVES 4

Mediterranean Lemon Chicken with Artichokes, Olives and Potato Bake

POTATO BAKE

- 4 potatoes, very thinly sliced
- 1 red onion, thinly sliced
- 125 g mature cheddar cheese, grated
- 1 cup cream
- 2 tsp flour
- 1 clove garlic, crushed
- salt and pepper, to taste
- ½ cup grated Parmesan

LEMON CHICKEN

- 4 butterflied chicken breasts
- ½ cup milk, in a flat plate
- 4 Tbs flour
- 2 Tbs fresh thyme leaves
- salt and freshly ground black pepper
- olive oil, for shallow frying

ARTICHOKE AND OLIVE TOPPING

- 1 × 400 g can artichoke hearts, cut into thirds
- 60 g pitted black olives, roughly chopped
- ½ cup roughly chopped Italian parsley
- 1 red pepper, cubed and lightly fried
- zest and juice of 1 lemon
- 2 Tbs olive oil
- 1 clove garlic, crushed

Make the potato bake first. Preheat the oven 180 °C. Layer the potatoes, onion and cheddar cheese, seasoning each layer lightly.

Mix the cream, flour and garlic together and season lightly. Pour over the potatoes and sprinkle with the Parmesan cheese.

Bake for 45 to 60 minutes, till the potatoes are tender.

To prepare the chicken, dip the butterflied breasts in the milk. Mix the flour and thyme together and season with salt and pepper. Dip the damp chicken breasts into the flour and dust both sides. Lay them onto a flat tray till ready to fry.

Mix all the topping ingredients together lightly and set aside in a small saucepan till you are ready to serve.

When the potatoes are nearly ready, pan-fry the chicken in olive oil. Just before you have finished cooking the last chicken breast, warm the artichoke mixture on the stove.

To serve, spoon some potato bake onto each plate, top with chicken and finish off with some artichoke and olive topping. Serve immediately.

SERVES 4

My desire to taste Greece came from my first mouthful of meltingly chewy, deep-fried haloumi cheese. When I was young, the Pappas children were my friends (they still are) and while they were all playing together outside I would wander into the kitchen. Their grandmother, a tiny woman dressed in black from head to toe, would lure me indoors with the tantalising aromas of tomato and oregano coming from her delicious kitchen. And there I would be, begging for a taste with my eyes. She spoke almost no English, but she knew I wanted to be fed. I remember a steaming pot of fish soup, moussaka coming out of the oven, all bubbling and golden, freshly baked herbed bread and salty, chalky feta cheese.

Savoury Greek Bread-and-butter Pudding

- 8 slices buttered bread, halved

FILLING
- 3 cups cooked spinach
- 1 onion, chopped and cooked in butter
- 200 g feta cheese, crumbled
- 1 cup fresh cream
- 1 cup milk
- 4 eggs, beaten
- ¼ tsp ground nutmeg
- freshly ground black pepper
- 1 Tbs chopped dill
- 1 tsp dried oregano
- 2 tsp lemon zest
- 2 cloves garlic, crushed
- ½ cup grated Parmesan

GARNISHING
- 2 Tbs grated Parmesan
- 10 cherry tomatoes, halved
- 10 black olives
- fresh rosemary sprigs
- 1 small red onion, thinly sliced

This recipe is for my friends Michael, Tony, Andrew and Dianne Pappas.

Preheat the oven to 180 °C. Butter the base of a deep oven-proof dish. Place a layer of bread onto the base of the dish.

Mix together the filling ingredients, and spoon half onto the bread slices. Top with another layer of bread and finish by spooning over the rest of the filling.

Press the top down to level it and let it stand for 20 minutes. Sprinkle the garnishing over the top and bake till puffed up and golden; about 30 to 40 minutes.

Serve hot with a salad.

SERVES 4

I adore natural Greek yoghurt; so thick, velvety, silky-rich and creamy. I couldn't get enough of it while I was in Greece and couldn't bear the thought of never being able to eat it again, so I brought a large tub home with me to use as a starter to make my own yoghurt over and over again. This I did for many years and always made sure I kept a jar or two back to start the next batch. But sadly 'someone' licked those two jars clean without asking and that put paid to my Greek yoghurt! I would drain my yoghurt and it would end up so thick you could cut it with a knife. It was heavenly drenched in honey and topped with toasted walnuts, or served savoury as *tzatziki* à la Jenny.

Tzatziki

- 1 litre natural or Greek yoghurt
- 2 cups diced English cucumber
- 12 fresh mint leaves, rolled and thinly sliced
- 3 cloves garlic, well crushed
- 1 Tbs chopped fresh coriander
- 1 Tbs chopped fresh dill
- 2 tsp fresh ripe lemon zest
- lemon juice, to taste
- 1 Tbs extra virgin olive oil
- salt and freshly ground black pepper

Line a sieve with muslin cloth, or a very new tea towel, and pour the yoghurt into it. Let it drain till it is nice and thick.

Stir the remaining ingredients together so that the flavours can mingle, and chill in the fridge till needed.

Remove the thickened yoghurt from the sieve, stir it into the herb mixture and serve with freshly baked flat bread.

SERVES 4 TO 6

Oregano and Olive Loaf

- 4 cups cake flour
- 2 tsp salt
- 4 tsp sugar
- 10 g instant yeast
- 1 Tbs olive oil
- 1½ cups lukewarm water
- 1 tsp dried oregano
- 1 cup pitted black olives, halved

Preheat the oven to 200 °C. Place all the dry ingredients into a bowl and make a well in the centre. Add the oil and three-quarters of the water and mix it in to form a soft dough. Add a little more water if need be, or a small amount of flour if it is too wet.

Knead the dough until it is smooth and elastic to the touch; about 15 minutes. Place the dough back into the bowl and oil the top. Cover with a clean cloth and place it in a warm place to rise to twice its size.

Remove the dough from the bowl. Mix together the oregano and chopped olives, and knead into the dough. Place your dough onto a floured baking tray, shape your bread, dust with flour and leave it to rise to twice its size.

Bake in the oven for about 35 to 40 minutes, or until the crust is crisp and the loaf sounds hollow when tapped.

Remove and cool before slicing. This bread is very good served with tzatziki (see recipe opposite).

TIP: Let all the steam escape and you will have a lighter loaf, so don't cut the bread straight from the oven – let it cool down first!

MAKES 1 LARGE LOAF

Walnuts, oranges, yoghurt and honey always make me think of Greece and the yummy sticky cakes and cookies I ate there. The waiter at our hotel in Glyfada used to bring this to the table as a little something extra on the side. Ha! He never got to have any though, the charmer!

Yoghurt Cake with Walnuts and Orange Syrup

YOGHURT CAKE

- 1 cup oil
- 1½ cups castor sugar
- 5 eggs, separated
- 1 tsp vanilla essence
- 1 cup natural yoghurt
- 3¾ cups self-raising flour, sifted
- 1 cup chopped, toasted walnuts
- finely grated zest of 1 orange

ORANGE SYRUP

- 1½ cups white sugar
- ½ cup hot water
- ½ cup freshly squeezed lemon juice
- 1 cup freshly squeezed orange juice
- 2 cardamom pods, split

Preheat the oven to 180 °C and grease a 23 cm round cake tin. Beat the oil and sugar together until light and fluffy, and then beat the egg yolks in one at a time. Set aside. Mix the vanilla essence into the yoghurt.

Now, alternately mix the flour and yoghurt into the egg mixture. Don't over-mix! Stir in the walnuts and orange zest.

Whisk the egg whites till soft peaks form, and gently fold into the cake mixture. Pour into the cake tin and bake on the middle shelf in the oven for 50 to 60 minutes, until a skewer inserted into the centre of the cake comes out clean. Poke holes into the top of the cake with a skewer.

Heat all the orange syrup ingredients together gently till the sugar has dissolved. Place the cake on a wire rack with a plate underneath to catch the drips, and pour over the warm syrup.

Serve with big blobs of mascarpone or Greek yoghurt.

MAKES 1 CAKE

TURKEY

I loved Istanbul where snapdragons with enormous shocking-pink heads grew out of every crack and crevice around the old ruined buildings. I became weak from the heady perfume that hit me when I passed a flower cart overflowing with huge, spicy carnations, luscious stocks, delicately scented sweet peas and the most fragrant roses I have ever smelled. They left me feeling intoxicated!

My first breakfast in Turkey nearly drove me mad too. How do you make a decision when you have so many dishes to choose from? Freshly baked Turkish breads and pastries dripping with honey and encrusted with almost emerald green roughly chopped pistachio nuts. Anchovies and octopus marinated in olive oil, and various spreads and dips made from roasted red peppers, brinjals and olives. A selection of freshly chopped tomatoes, juicy cucumber and the crispest cos lettuce made their way to the table; and so did a bowl of beautiful freshly picked mint, dill, parsley and coriander to enhance each bite. There was a truly delicious dish made from eggs and peppers, garlic, tomatoes and cheese. Then I fell in love with the green beans in olive oil – these would make an Imam faint, never mind the brinjals that made him swoon – and a lentil soup, thick and ever so tasty. There were enormous wooden frames holding whole honey combs just waiting to be sliced; huge bowls of swollen sticky dates and fat soft and chewy sticky-sweet dried figs. It was a meal I won't ever forget.

And then there was our feast at a fish restaurant on the banks of a river. We had a wonderful view of the boats bobbing up and down at their moorings, and the moon was all bright and silver, lighting up the water and making it shimmer. We started our dinner with an array of little dishes that covered the whole table: so many, but I remember in particular the succulent mackerel in olive oil; the heavenly little plates of labneh cheese drenched with the peppery local olive oil and chopped herbs; the fragrant bowls of homemade aïoli and fat butter beans with a tomato and olive oil sauce.

It's hard to believe that we made it to the main courses but we managed to do justice to whole grilled sea bream with calamari and mussels, and heavenly *borek* – little pastries filled with cheese and potatoes. When you visit Turkey, you remember every mouthful you have tasted.

Ala Kilise
Ala Church
Bezirhane
The Old Oil Fabrik

We had this *kiymali pide* as part of a traditional Turkish buffet, and I must say I really liked it. I watched fascinated as the *pide* chef worked his dough on the marble worktop to make traditional Turkish pizza; they looked like little rowing boats topped with yummy fillings. He put them into the hell-hot wood-burning oven and I didn't have to wait long; the delicious smell told me they would soon be ready.

Turkish Pizza – *Kiymali Pide*

THE DOUGH

- 5 cups flour, sifted
- 10 g instant yeast
- 1 tsp salt
- 1 tsp sugar
- 3 eggs (keep 1 yolk for glazing)
- 4 Tbs melted butter
- 2 Tbs milk

THE FILLING

- 2 Tbs olive oil
- 1 onion, finely chopped
- 300 g lamb mince
- 3 cloves garlic
- 1 red pepper, diced
- 1 chilli, chopped
- 1 small brinjal, diced
- 1 tomato, diced
- salt and pepper
- 1 tsp paprika
- 1 tsp ground cumin
- ½ cup parsley, chopped
- ½ cup coriander, chopped
- 150 g feta cheese, crumbled

To make the dough, mix the flour, yeast, salt and sugar in a bowl. Beat together the eggs (set one of the yolks aside for later) with the butter and milk. Stir the mixture into the flour and then knead till you have nice soft dough; about 10 minutes.

Place in an oiled bowl and leave to rise to twice its size. Preheat the oven to 220 °C.

Divide the dough into six balls and press them out on a floured surface into circles about ½ cm thick. Place the circles, ready to be filled, onto floured baking trays.

For the filling, heat the oil in a saucepan. Fry the onion till almost golden, add the lamb, garlic and red pepper, and stir until the meat is cooked through. Stir in the chilli, brinjal and tomato, season with salt and pepper, and add the paprika and cumin. Cook gently till the tomato breaks up. Stir in the herbs and cool the mixture down.

Divide the filling and feta into six portions. Place a line of feta down the centre of each dough circle, and top with some filling, pressing it down. Roll in the edges of the dough to shape a boat, pressing the points together (an elongated oval). Brush with the beaten egg yolk mixed with a teaspoon of olive oil. Bake for 15 to 20 minutes.

SERVES 6

Yoghurt and Cucumber Soup – *Cacik*

YOGHURT SOUP
- 1 English cucumber, peeled and grated
- 3 cups natural yoghurt
- ¼ cup water
- 2 cloves garlic, crushed
- ¼ cup chopped fresh dill
- 2 Tbs chopped fresh mint
- salt, to taste
- freshly ground black pepper
- extra virgin olive oil
- paprika

JENNY'S EXTRAS (OPTIONAL)
- ½ cup chopped toasted walnuts
- ½ cup sultanas
- 3 spring onions with tops, chopped

This delicious chilled yoghurt and cucumber soup is very versatile and is central to the meze table in Turkey. Pronounced 'jajuk', cacik *can also be served as a dip or sauce with roasted meats or grilled vegetables. I like to add a few extras of my own, even though I know the Turks would have my guts for garters!*

Place the cucumber, yoghurt, water and crushed garlic in a bowl. Add the dill and mint, and season with salt and pepper to taste. I stir the optional extras into the soup at this point and let it chill till I am ready to serve it.

Spoon the well-chilled soup into serving bowls, drizzle with some olive oil and dust with paprika.

SERVES 4

Baby Marrow Fritters – *Kabak Mücveri*

- 400 g large baby marrows, grated, salted, rinsed and drained
- 1 onion, grated
- 100 g ricotta cheese
- 100 g feta cheese
- 1 tomato, deseeded and diced
- 3 Tbs parsley, chopped
- 3 Tbs dill, chopped
- 1 Tbs mint, chopped
- ¾ cup fresh breadcrumbs
- salt and pepper, to taste
- 2 eggs, beaten
- oil for shallow frying
- flour, for dusting

I discovered these tasty baby marrow fritters in Cappadocia on the buffet at our hotel. What a find! Delicious and very moreish, they also make for a great veggie burger.

Place the baby marrows, onion, ricotta, feta, tomato and herbs into a bowl with the breadcrumbs, and season with salt and pepper. Stir in the eggs and shape into patties – add more egg if needed.

Heat the oil. Dust the patties with flour and shallow-fry on both sides till golden. Serve with a yoghurt sauce such as *cacik* (see opposite for recipe).

SERVES 4 TO 6

While we were in Cappadocia we had an amazing lunch in a little restaurant run by a Turkish family: mother, father and two sons – when they weren't at school.

Outside their kitchen was a weathered stone fireplace used for baking bread and making Turkish pizza, and some plump happy chickens pecked away nearby – we were told that they were the best layers in Turkey and that they would never go hungry as long as they kept providing eggs.

We sat in this rustic setting in the shade of the vines and a large walnut tree, enjoying the fragrant, velvety roses that grew all around us. In Turkey there are roses everywhere, even on the sidewalks.

The mother was warm and friendly and let me join her at the stove while she prepared our lunch. She said it was called *menemen*, a simple dish of free-range eggs and organic tomatoes, peppers and chilli, which she made in individual metal bowls. I so loved these bowls that I bought them from her at the asking price. Once you have tasted this simple dish, you'll never forget it. The flavour is outstanding. Lunch was served with bowls of freshly picked lettuce and herbs, and some smoky bread fresh from the wood oven.

She told me that in their region all the food was prepared from fresh ingredients that were mostly organically grown. Her own little plot had a beautiful herb garden with all the basic herbs that are used almost daily in Turkish food; oregano, marjoram and thyme grew like wild fire, and then there were dill, parsley, mint and coriander. She grew some beautiful lettuces, tomatoes, baby marrows and spring onions too.

She also had a walnut tree and a cherry tree, and some grapes, oranges and pomegranates. She said that they would always start the day with a glass of freshly squeezed orange and pomegranate juice when it was in season – that was their secret to good health!

Eggs, Tomatoes and Peppers – *Menemen*

- 8 eggs
- salt and pepper, to taste
- ½ cup olive oil
- 2 onions, cut into rings
- 3 green peppers, diced
- 6 large tomatoes, roughly chopped
- 1 red chilli, chopped
- 2 cloves garlic, crushed
- flat leaf parsley, for garnishing

Beat the eggs in a bowl and season with salt and pepper. Heat the olive oil in a large pan, and then gently fry the onions and peppers for three minutes without browning them. Add the tomatoes, chilli and garlic, season to taste and cook till the tomatoes are soft and the liquid has reduced by half.

Pour the eggs into the centre of the pan and slowly stir into the tomato mixture. Keep stirring slowly until it begins to firm. Remove from the heat.

Garnish with some flat leaf parsley and serve with crusty bread; great for mopping up juices!

SERVES 4

Bean Dip - *Fava*

BEAN DIP
- 175 g dried broad (fava) beans
- 2 garlic cloves, crushed
- 1½ Tbs lemon juice
- 1 tsp tahini or sesame oil
- ⅓ cup olive oil
- salt and pepper, to taste
- ½ tsp ground cumin
- large pinch paprika
- flat bread, to serve

GARNISHING
- spring onion, thinly sliced
- 1 tsp chopped preserved lemon
- 1 Tbs chopped coriander
- 2 Tbs chopped flat leaf parsley
- 2 Tbs toasted sesame seeds

Soak the beans overnight, remove the skins and simmer over medium heat till soft; approximately one hour. Make sure that you do not add salt to the water as the beans will not soften. Remove the lid and cook for a further 15 minutes, or until most of the liquid has evaporated.

Purée the beans in a food processor, adding the garlic, lemon juice, tahini and olive oil, and blend to a thick smooth paste. Transfer to a bowl, season to taste and add the cumin and paprika. Stir in the garnishing ingredients and serve with flat bread.

TIP: This dip can be served at room temperature or chilled.

SERVES 4

The Turks make the most delicious full fat cream cheese. At breakfast I would top it with rosy quince compote. What an amazing mouthful!

Labneh

- 2 litres thick Greek yoghurt
- ⅓ cup extra virgin olive oil
- 2 tsp salt
- freshly ground black pepper
- juice of 1 lemon
- rind of 1 lemon, thinly sliced
- 1 bay leaf
- 1 tsp toasted cumin seeds
- 2 large sprigs fresh thyme
- 2 sprigs rosemary
- 1 red chilli
- extra virgin olive oil, to top up jar

Labneh is a creamy yoghurt cheese that is found throughout Turkey. The longer you drain the yoghurt, the thicker the cheese will be.

Mix the yoghurt with the olive oil, salt and pepper, and lemon juice and rind. Stir together well.

Line a colander with muslin cloth and pour in the yoghurt. Pull up the side of the cloth and tie firmly – it should look like a money bag. Hang the yoghurt for two days in a cool place or in the fridge if the weather is hot. Put a bowl underneath to catch the liquid as it strains.

After the two days are up, remove the thickened yoghurt from the muslin; roll it into walnut-sized balls and layer them in a large jar with the herbs, spices and chilli. Cover with olive oil.

Let the labneh marinate for a minimum of five days before eating it. They are good for two weeks to a month if refrigerated.

Serve with a dusting of paprika and a scattering of very finely chopped garlic and parsley.

TIP: Use any leftover oil to dress salads. The oil may solidify from being in the fridge, but let it stand at room temperature for a few minutes and it will soon liquefy.

MAKES ABOUT 1 KG

One of my culinary highlights when I visited Turkey was in Istanbul where we had a breakfast feast at the Ciragan Palace Kempinski Hotel. I was ravenous when I arrived but was completely overwhelmed by the huge selection of food that could just as easily have been served at lunch or dinner. I made a brave stab at the display and soon discovered this delicious Turkish bulgur wheat salad. I just loved it – I could have eaten it all day – and to my great delight I found it on the mezze bar for the duration of our stay.

Turkish Bulgur Wheat Salad – *Kisir*

- 300 g cherry tomatoes
- 2 large red peppers, quartered and deseeded
- 1 tsp paprika
- 3 cloves garlic, peeled
- ½ cup olive oil
- salt and black pepper, to taste
- 2 cups bulgur wheat
- 2 cups boiling water
- ½ tsp salt
- 3 Tbs lemon juice
- 1 cup fresh Italian parsley, chopped
- ½ cup fresh mint leaves, chopped
- 1 large tomato, seeded and diced
- 4 spring onions with green tops, chopped
- black pepper
- ¼ tsp cayenne pepper

Preheat the oven to 200 °C. Toss the cherry tomatoes, red peppers, paprika, garlic and olive oil together and season with salt and pepper. Spread out on a baking tray and roast for 20 minutes or until the tomatoes are wrinkly. Remove from the oven and blend till smooth.

Place the bulgur wheat, along with the boiling water and half a teaspoon of salt, in a bowl and let it rest for 30 minutes, absorbing the water. Fluff it up with two forks and toss in the remaining ingredients.

Stir in the tomato and pepper purée, taste and adjust the seasoning if necessary. Refrigerate until you are ready to serve.

SERVES 6

Brinjals with Olive Oil and Tomato Sauce – *Şakşuka*

- 3 long, firm brinjals
- 2 Tbs extra virgin olive oil
- 3 green peppers, diced
- 2 tomatoes, grated
- 1 tsp tomato paste
- 2 to 3 cloves garlic, crushed
- salt and pepper
- chopped parsley
- extra olive oil

Cut the brinjals into four lengthways, then cut into 2 cm chunks. Degorge the bitter juices by sprinkling with salt then leaving to drain for 15 minutes. Wash and pat dry.

Heat some olive oil in a frying pan and fry the brinjals till golden; drain on paper towels and set aside.

Add more oil to the pan and sauté the peppers for two minutes, and then add the tomatoes and tomato paste. Cook for six minutes, stir in the garlic, season with salt and pepper, and remove from the heat.

Pour the sauce over the brinjals, scatter with parsley and drizzle with olive oil. Serve immediately.

SERVES 4

Brinjals stuffed with Aromatic Spiced Lamb – *Karniyarik*

- 6 medium-size brinjals, with stem cap on
- 2 Tbs olive oil
- 1 green pepper, finely diced
- 1 large onion, finely diced
- 4 cloves garlic, crushed
- 1 tsp ground cumin
- 1 tsp fresh thyme leaves
- 200 g minced lamb, beef or chicken
- 3 tomatoes, skinned and chopped
- salt and pepper, to taste
- 2 Tbs unsalted butter, melted
- ¾ cup chicken stock
- grated Parmesan, for garnishing
- chopped parsley, for garnishing

This is my twist on a meal we enjoyed in Istanbul.

Preheat the oven to 180 °C. Peel the brinjals leaving three strips of skin on each one for presentation. Do not remove the stem caps. Now make a deep lengthwise incision with a sharp knife into one side of each brinjal, starting a little way down from the stem and stopping before you reach the bottom, taking care not to slice them right through.

Place the brinjals in a bowl that fits them and sprinkle with two teaspoons of salt, cover with lukewarm water and let them soak for 30 minutes.

While the brinjals are soaking, heat the olive oil in a saucepan and gently fry the green pepper, onion and garlic for three minutes. Add the cumin and thyme, cook for two minutes and then add the lamb mince and cook for six minutes while stirring. Once the meat takes on some colour, add the chopped tomatoes, season with salt and pepper, and simmer gently till most of the sauce has reduced.

Give the brinjals some attention now. Remove them from their brine bath and give them a squeeze to remove the brine and dry them out a little. Brush them with melted butter and in a hot pan gently brown them on all sides in batches. Remove and cool.

Place the cooled brinjals onto a flat surface slit-side up and stuff each one with minced lamb. Pack them into an oven-proof dish, pour the chicken stock into the dish, cover with foil and bake in the preheated oven for 30 minutes or until soft and tender.

Garnish with grated Parmesan cheese and chopped parsley. Serve drizzled with extra olive oil, chunks of freshly baked bread, a bowl of herbs and salad leaves, and wedges of freshly cut lemon.

TIP: The herb bowl should contain fresh rocket, dill, mint, parsley and coriander.

SERVES 6

You can't visit Istanbul without going on a river cruise. We took a long, leisurely cruise on the Bosphorus River, enjoying the magnificent view of the bridge and the mosque. When we disembarked, we mingled with the locals on the wharf of the Eminonu harbour. They were queuing to get their hands on the Famous Turkish Fried Fish Sandwich: a noisy crisp freshly baked baguette filled with cos lettuce, rocket, mint, chillies, freshly fried fish, mayonnaise and sun-ripened tomatoes, with a wedge of lemon on the side. They sat on low boxes at makeshift tables of crates, chomping away and almost humming with pleasure as they wolfed down their delicious feast.

I loved how local families came to the bridge over the Bosphorus River: fathers and sons, daughters and mothers, all fishing together over the side. What an amazing family outing, and with a bountiful catch for dinner for most of them!

Famous Fish Sandwich

- 4 × 200 g portions firm-fleshed fish
- salt and freshly ground black pepper
- cornflour for dusting
- oil for frying
- 4 crispy rolls or baguettes, split and buttered
- 2 fresh crisp cos lettuces
- 1 red onion, sliced
- 200 g wild rocket
- sundried tomatoes (optional)
- fresh mint (optional)
- fresh dill (optional)
- mayonnaise (optional)
- lemon wedges

Season the fish and then dust lightly with cornflour. Heat the oil in a large frying pan and fry the fish till golden on both sides; about four to five minutes per side.

Fill each baguette with a selection of the remaining ingredients and a slice of fish. Squeeze over the juice from a wedge of freshly cut lemon, and munch away!

SERVES 4

Döner kebab restaurants line the pavements of Istanbul, sending spicy aromas out into the street to entice you to eat even though you aren't hungry! The döner kebabs are made from meat roasted on a vertical spit, and these spicy skewers remind me of their tempting fragrance.

Spicy Turkish Shish Kebabs – *Şiş Kebap*

- 3 cloves garlic, crushed
- 4 Tbs olive oil
- ½ tsp dried crushed chilli
- 1 tsp paprika
- 2 tsp ground cumin
- 1 tsp ground coriander
- 1.2 kg deboned lamb leg, cubed
- salt and freshly ground black pepper
- 8 pre-soaked wooden skewers
- 16 fresh bay leaves

Place the garlic, oil, chilli, paprika, cumin and coriander into a bowl big enough to hold the meat. Give it a good mix and add the lamb cubes, stirring well to coat. Cover with plastic wrap and leave to marinate for three hours or overnight.

Before threading the lamb onto the skewers season the cubes of meat with salt and pepper. Divide up the lamb and thread it onto the skewers, adding two bay leaves to each skewer.

Grill over white-hot coals or in a very hot griddle pan. I like mine brown and crisp on the outside and slightly juicy on the inside. Serve with a white bean pâté, bread and a red onion salad.

TIP: To make the salad, toss slivers of red onions, tomatoes and black olives with chunks of freshly cut cucumber. Dress with olive oil, garlic and a splash freshly squeezed lemon juice.

SERVES 4

Deep-fried Mussels – *Midye Tava*

- 1 cup flour
- 10 g dried yeast
- 2 Tbs melted butter
- 2 eggs, separated
- ½ tsp salt
- pepper
- ½ tsp sugar
- ½ cup lukewarm water
- 2 spring onions, finely chopped
- oil, for deep frying
- 30 green-lipped mussels, meat only
- flour, for dusting

These huge, fat, juicy mussels were being cooked on the street and they were also being offered fresh, with a splash of lemon, to people passing by on the way to board a boat in the harbour.

Mix the flour and yeast in a bowl and make a well in the centre. Combine the melted butter with the egg yolks, salt, pepper and sugar, and stir in the water. Beat into the flour and let this rest for 10 minutes.

Whisk the egg whites till stiff peak forms, and fold into the batter. Stir in the spring onion.

Heat the oil in a deep pan. Dust the mussels with flour and dip into the batter. Deep-fry in batches till golden brown – a few at a time so that they aren't soggy.

Serve with wedges of fresh lemon.

SERVES 4 TO 6

I just fell in love with the little neighbourhood bakeries in Turkey. The windows were filled with displays of freshly baked breads of all shapes and sizes: puffed up and flat; hoop-shaped and encrusted with sesame seeds, round and long. There were also bright pink cakes and deliciously dense syrupy nutty bakes. And the tarts! This delicious tart is a celebration of the gorgeous cherries we ate in Turkey – huge, fleshy, dark and juicy.

Cherry and Almond Tart

THE CHERRIES

- 1.5 kg cherries, washed and stoned
- 1½ cups sugar
- juice of 1 lemon
- ½ cup brandy
- 2 tsp butter

PASTRY

- 100 g ground almonds
- ½ cup flour
- pinch salt
- 1 Tbs castor sugar
- 100 g cold butter, cut into blocks
- 1 egg yolk
- few teaspoons iced water, if needed

To prepare the filling, place the cherries in a saucepan with the sugar and lemon juice, and stir until the sugar dissolves. Simmer gently for 20 minutes.

Bring to the boil and let it bubble away for four minutes. Remove the cherries with a slotted spoon and reduce the liquid by a third. Stir in the brandy and cook for 30 seconds. Remove from the heat, stir in the butter and return the cherries to the pot. Leave to cool.

To make the pastry shell, place the almonds, flour, salt and castor sugar into the bowl of your food processor. Give it a turn to mix the dry ingredients, then add the butter and blitz till the mixture resembles breadcrumbs.

Stir in the egg to form soft dough, adding a little iced water if it is too dry. Close the dough in plastic wrap and chill for 30 minutes.

Roll out the pastry on a very lightly floured surface to no more than ½ cm thick and line your baking tin with it. It's important that you do not stretch the pastry or it will shrink during baking.

Tap the tin on a flat surface to get the pastry to settle in, trim the edges with a knife, and prick the pastry all over with a fork to ensure that there are no air pockets.

Rest the pastry for at least an hour before baking – this will help to prevent it from shrinking when you bake it.

Line the pastry with a circle of greaseproof paper a little larger than the tin so you can lift it out easily, and fill it with dried beans or raw rice. Bake at 170 °C to 175 °C for about 20 to 25 minutes – it must not brown. Remove from the oven, lift out the beans and baking paper. Brush the base with some beaten egg and bake for another five minutes to seal the base.

Remove from the oven and cool to room temperature. Spoon the cherries into the pastry case and bake at 180 °C for 25 to 30 minutes. Serve warm with lashings of cream.

MAKES 1 TART

The spice market in Istanbul was like an Aladdin's cave – fabrics, spices, fragrant flower oils, floral teas, silver and gold jewellery, leather bags and shoes, pottery and beautiful candle holders made from colourful glass. But my best discovery was a Turkish delight shop just off the main walkway where I discovered huge quivering slabs of ruby-red pomegranate Turkish delight, studded with intensely green sliced pistachio nuts. Oh, what a sight! I don't think I will ever see anything so deliciously beautiful again.

Turkish Delight – *Lokum*

- ½ cup fresh pomegranate juice
- 3¾ cups sugar
- 50 g gelatine
- 1 Tbs rose water
- ¼ tsp red food colouring
- 100 g pistachio nuts, blanched and toasted
- ½ cup sifted icing sugar
- 1 Tbs cornflour

Place the pomegranate juice and sugar in a saucepan and heat gently. Sprinkle the gelatine over the surface and stir until the granules and sugar have dissolved. Boil gently for 10 minutes till nicely thickened.

Remove from the heat and stir in the rose water, food colouring and pistachio nuts.

Rinse a 20 cm shallow square tin with cold water, but don't dry it. Pour the mixture into the tin and tap the edges to even out and settle the mixture. Cover and leave to set and firm up at room temperature for no less than 12 hours.

Now mix together the icing sugar and cornflour. Place a piece of wax paper down onto a wooden board and dust with the icing sugar mixture.

Dust the top of the Turkish delight with some icing sugar and invert it onto the board. Dust with more icing sugar, and cover with another sheet of wax paper until you are ready to cut it into squares.

Cut the Turkish delight into squares using an oiled knife. I use almond or vegetable oil for this. Roll the squares into more icing sugar before storing in an airtight container.

You are welcome to use water instead of the pomegranate juice, in which case you will need a drop or two of pink food colouring. I like to make the Turkish delight in miniature bread tins then I can have slices instead of squares and expose more of the luscious centre! Invert in the same way as if you were making squares.

TIP: Never allow the mixture to boil until the last grain of sugar has dissolved. Make sure that you stir into all the nooks and corners as well as the base of your pot. Avoid splashing; be gentle.

MAKES ABOUT 40 LITTLE SQUARES

INDIA

Growing up in Durban, there was Indian food all around me; an Indian family lived next door to us and became very good friends, and there were several Indian traders in our neighbourhood. So knowing the cuisine and loving it, whenever I smell Indian food I want to eat it straightaway.

Miriam and her husband Omar ran a little greengrocer on the corner of the street where I lived. They started very early and ended late, and took all their meals at the back of the store where Miriam had set up a small space with a table and a two-plate stove. She had two young sons and her oldest son Imran played with my son Wade. He spent most of his time with me while they worked and my reward was cooking alongside Miriam a few times a week.

I loved watching and learning from Miriam as she enveloped my kitchen with aromas that filled me with a longing to taste India for real. She taught the magic of tempering and blending spices that would transform the simplest of ingredients into the most mouth-wateringly delicious dishes. She taught me that there was rice other than long-grain; I was introduced to basmati and she showed me how to cook it, plain or infused with saffron and cumin, curry leaves and coriander. She took plain yoghurt to new heights for me by stirring in toasted cumin, freshly chopped chillies, mint or coriander, grated carrots or cucumber to serve beside a dish. And she taught me that a curry could be made from vegetables and pulses and not just from meat alone.

One day we raided the two huge mango trees that grew in the parking lot of Sparks Corner where she had her shop. The mangoes were still green – perfect for making mango pickle and atchar, all hot spicy and sour.

My mouth waters every time I think of it …

I love travelling with my very dear friend Naushad Khan. We both have a passion for food and when we were in India together we spent our time happily eating and shopping.

We had the ultimate tandoori feast at the Bukhara restaurant in Delhi: giant prawns; tender succulent lamb; plump free-range chicken; yummy goat; and paneer, all smoky and spicy. The very proud restaurant manager was pleased to tell us that his tandoori dishes were the best in all of India.

Tandoori cooking originated in North Persia and is still very popular today. It derives its name from the distinctive cylindrical clay oven that is used to cook the food. The tandoor stands upright and is heated from the bottom by wood or charcoal that is burned within the oven itself. Unless you are lucky enough to have a tandoori oven, you will have to improvise and make do with your oven at home, but you can still enjoy the succulence and flavour of traditional tandoori dishes by using the same spices and by tenderising your meat in a yoghurt marinade.

Tandoori Chicken

TANDOORI MARINADE

- 1 cup natural yoghurt
- juice of 1 lemon
- 2 drops red food colouring
- 2 drops yellow food colouring
- 1 Tbs grated ginger
- 4 cloves garlic, grated
- ¼ tsp ground cloves
- ¼ tsp ground cardamom
- 1 tsp ground cinnamon
- 1 tsp ground coriander
- 1 tsp ground cumin
- 1 tsp paprika
- ½ tsp chilli powder

CHICKEN

- 1 really big free-range chicken, 2 kg or more
- salt and pepper, to taste
- 1 Tbs melted butter

You must mimic the bright orangey-red colour of tandoori chicken by mixing a few drops of red and yellow food colouring with your yoghurt. Get yourself a nice big free-range chicken to make this dish. I normally marinate the chicken the night before I need it.

Stir all the ingredients together for the marinade and set it aside while you prepare the chicken. Make three slashes on each breast with a sharp knife and two slashes on each leg. Push down hard on the breast bone till you hear it crack. Place the chicken in a glass bowl, rub the marinade into the slashes and make sure that the bird is completely covered with the yoghurt mix. Cover the bowl with plastic wrap and refrigerate for at least six hours, or overnight.

Preheat the oven to 200 °C. Place the chicken on an oven rack above an oven tray to catch the drips. Season with salt and pepper, dab with melted butter and roast for 40 minutes.

Spoon over the juices from the drip tray and the turn the heat up to 220 °C and return the chicken to the oven, roasting for another 20 minutes. To test whether the chicken is ready, prick the thigh (which is the thickest part) and when the juices run clear, take it out of the oven.

Let it rest for 10 to 15 minutes before carving, and serve with roti and a simple salad. I usually toss together some tomatoes, cucumber, coriander, chillies and red onion, all dressed with a lemon vinaigrette.

SERVES 4 TO 6

I have eaten roti in many places in the world, from India to Singapore, but I have never had any as light, buttery and crispy as this one. Miriam gave me my first roti board and I have never stopped using it.

Roti

- ½ cup cake flour
- ¼ tsp salt
- 1 Tbs ice-cold water
- butter at room temperature, for spreading
- vegetable oil or ghee, for frying

Mix the flour, salt and water to form a soft but not sticky dough. If the dough is too sticky then dust it with flour and work it as you would knead bread. Wrap in plastic wrap and rest for about 10 minutes.

On a lightly floured surface, roll the dough out to a thin round. Spread the surface of the dough with a thickish layer of butter and roll the dough up into a snake shape. Roll the snake into a coil and rest in the refrigerator for about 20 minutes.

Now roll the dough out to a thickness of 3 to 4 mm. In a frying pan large enough to hold the roti, heat a little oil on medium heat. (I normally just put the roti straight into a hot pan to save a few calories.) Slide the roti into the pan and fry till golden brown on one side, then turn over and cook the other side. Serve nice and hot.

TIP: If you are making more than one roti, interleave with greaseproof paper. They can be made a few hours ahead. In that case, reheat in a 140 °C oven for a few minutes before serving.

MAKES 1 LARGE ROTI

One of the quick and easy meals Miriam and I would make was roti and kabobs; spicy lamb or beef meatballs with a delicious tomato-based gravy that became a firm favourite for lunch on a Saturday.

Roti and Kabobs

KABOBS
- 1 kg lean minced lamb or beef
- 1 small onion, grated
- 1 tsp grated ginger
- 2 cloves garlic, grated
- 2 Tbs freshly chopped coriander
- 2 Tbs freshly chopped mint
- 1 small green chilli, deseeded and chopped
- 3 Tbs chickpea flour, or chilli bite mix
- ¼ tsp ground white pepper
- 1 tsp ground coriander
- 2 tsp ground cumin
- ½ tsp salt
- ¼ tsp turmeric
- 3 Tbs natural yoghurt

TOMATO GRAVY
- 2 Tbs vegetable oil
- 1 onion, finely chopped
- ½ tsp ground cinnamon
- 1 tsp black mustard seeds
- 1 tsp ground cumin
- 3 curry leaves
- 2 cloves garlic, finely chopped
- 2 green chillies, cut lengthways and deseeded
- 1.5 kg tomatoes, grated
- juice of 1 lemon
- salt and pepper
- freshly chopped coriander

Place all the kabob ingredients in a bowl and give them a thorough mix to incorporate all the bits and pieces. Chill the mixture for 30 minutes and then roll into 24 meatballs.

Heat a little vegetable oil in a frying pan and fry the meatballs in batches till lightly browned but not cooked all the way through. Set aside and make the gravy.

Heat the oil in a saucepan, add the onion and cook stirring for two minutes. Add the cinnamon, mustard seeds, cumin, curry leaves, garlic and chillies, and cook stirring for four minutes.

Stir in the tomatoes, lemon juice, salt and pepper, and add the meatballs. Simmer till the tomatoes are cooked down, adding a little warm water if the sauce is cooking down too fast.

Stir in the coriander and serve with roti and sambals on the side.

TIP: The sambals featured on page 151 would work very well as accompaniments for this dish.

SERVES 4 TO 6

I just love the silky flesh of brinjals. I sometimes make this curry with minced beef and serve it with roti, so everyone gets to make their own Indian wrap.

Lamb, Brinjal and Butter Bean Curry

CURRY

- 2 large long firm brinjals, cubed
- 3 Tbs vegetable oil
- 3 Tbs unsalted butter
- 3 large onions, thinly sliced
- 5 cm piece fresh ginger, grated
- 1 Tbs coriander seeds, toasted and ground
- 1 Tbs cumin seeds, toasted and ground
- 5 cardamom pods, toasted and ground
- 1 tsp turmeric
- 2 tsp chilli powder
- 1 fresh green chilli, slit
- 1.5 kg lean cubed lamb or lamb knuckle
- 2 large ripe tomatoes, chopped
- 10 cloves garlic, crushed
- salt, to taste
- about 1½ cups boiling water
- ¾ tsp ground cinnamon
- 2 cups cooked butter beans
- 10 curry leaves (optional)
- 3 Tbs chopped fresh coriander

RAITA

- 2 cups thick Greek yoghurt
- 1 medium English cucumber, washed
- 1 tsp roasted ground cumin
- 1 Tbs chopped fresh mint
- 1 Tbs chopped fresh coriander
- 2 tsp fresh lemon juice
- salt, to taste

To make the curry, salt the brinjal cubes and let them sweat for 20 minutes. Rinse under cold water and pat dry. Heat two tablespoons of oil in a large frying pan and brown the brinjals lightly – don't cook them completely. Set aside till needed.

Heat the butter and one tablespoon of oil in a large saucepan, add the onions and let them cook gently till they reduce down to two-thirds of their original size. Add a few drops of water if need be to stop them from burning.

Now stir in the ginger, ground coriander, cumin, cardamom, turmeric and chilli powder, and cook stirring for a few minutes to release the fragrance of the spices, adding a few spoonfuls of warm water at a time to stop them from burning.

Stir in the fresh chilli and lamb, and cook for five minutes. Don't let it stick. Add the tomatoes and garlic, season with salt and cover with a lid, simmering for 20 minutes. Lift the lid and add the boiling water, just enough to cover the lamb, and stir in the cinnamon. Simmer till the lamb is tender; about 50 to 60 minutes.

While the curry is simmering away, make the raita. Place the yoghurt in a bowl. Peel half of the cucumber and chop very finely. Dice the other half (with the skin on) and stir all the cucumber into the yoghurt with the cumin, mint, coriander and lemon juice. Season with salt and add a little more cumin if you like. Set aside in the fridge until needed.

Just before you are ready to serve, add the beans, brinjals and curry leaves to the lamb, and cook till warmed through. Stir in the fresh coriander and serve with roti (see recipe on page 146) or steamed rice, and the cucumber and mint raita. The sambals featured on page 151 would also be good with this dish.

TIP: Cook the onions nice and slow till they cook right down. The sugars cook out of them this way, giving you an amazing curry.

SERVES 4 TO 6

Garam Masala

- 8 cardamom pods
- 1 tsp black peppercorns
- 1 tsp white peppercorns
- 2 Tbs cumin seeds
- ½ tsp cloves
- 2 bay leaves, shredded
- 2 cinnamon sticks, halved
- 1 Tbs coriander seeds

Heat a frying pan till it is really hot. Place all the spices into the pan and keep stirring till the aroma is released. Do not burn!

Remove the spice mixture from the pan to cool, then grind or pound to a powder. Keep in an airtight container.

TIP: This garam masala works particularly well with meat and poultry.

When I first started cooking with Miriam I used to think she was sneaking something into the pot without telling me. Some cooks do that you know. They leave something out of the recipe so that your dish is never quite the same as theirs. She was weak with laughter at the thought. She said that all Indian cooks add a little garam masala near the end of cooking to lend a spicy fragrance to the dish before serving. She always grated a little nutmeg into the dish at the end.

'Garam masala' means 'hot mixture' and Miriam would make up a different blend for beef, chicken, lamb, fish and vegetables. She dry-roasted the spices before grinding them, and she only made enough to last two weeks. She would seal them up tight so that they would be fresh and fragrant when it was time to use them. She said that as she would never ever buy garam masala herself, I should learn to make it too. There is no authentic mixture readily available in the shops and every Indian household has a bottle filled with a special blend of its own.

She used to make a basic mixture with whole black and white peppercorns, bay leaves, nutmeg, cloves, cinnamon, cumin seeds and cardamom pods, all toasted before they were ground to release their divine aromas and flavour.

Red Onion and Minted Yoghurt Salad

- 1 cup washed and shredded fresh mint
- 1 large green or red chilli, chopped
- 1½ cups natural yoghurt
- a really good grind of sea salt
- juice of 1 lemon
- ¼ cup water, if needed
- 1 small red onion, very thinly sliced and lightly salted
- 1 tsp toasted bashed cumin seeds

Place the mint into the bowl of a food processor and whizz till it is finely chopped. Add the chilli and yoghurt, and blend till well incorporated. Season with salt, add the lemon juice and blend again till smooth. Thin out the sauce with a little water if needed.

Pour the yoghurt mix onto the onion slices and stir in the cumin seeds. Let the sauce rest for an hour before eating it.

TIP: It is delicious served with all grilled meats, fish, curries and roasted chicken.

SERVES 4

Fresh Tomato Sambal

- 3 firm ripe tomatoes, diced
- 1 medium carrot, peeled and roughly grated
- 1 small red onion, diced
- 1 clove garlic, grated
- 2 green fresh chillies, thinly sliced
- salt, to taste
- ¼ cup freshly chopped coriander
- 1 Tbs red or white wine vinegar

If you don't want this to be too hot, remove the chilli seeds before slicing.

Toss all the ingredients together, adjust the seasoning and chill till needed. This sambal is a refreshing accompaniment to curries.

TIP: Rub a little olive oil onto your hands to act as a barrier before slicing the chillies; this way you can wash away the heat!

SERVES 4

Spicy Fish Cakes with Minted Chilli Drizzle

MINTED CHILLI DRIZZLE
- 1 cup natural yoghurt
- 1 clove garlic, chopped
- 2 Tbs chopped mint
- ½ tsp ground cumin
- 1 Tbs lemon juice
- 1 tsp lemon zest
- salt, to taste

SPICY FISH CAKES
- ¼ tsp turmeric
- ¼ tsp ground cumin
- ¼ tsp ground coriander
- ¼ tsp ground chilli power
- 1 Tbs water
- 2 Tbs oil
- 1 onion, finely chopped
- 2 cloves garlic, crushed
- 300 g cooked mashed potato
- 500 g hake, lightly steamed and flaked
- 2 Tbs freshly chopped coriander
- salt and pepper, to taste
- flour for dusting
- 1 egg, beaten
- 1 ½ cups fresh breadcrumbs
- oil for shallow frying

Place all the ingredients for the chilli drizzle into the bowl of your food processor and blitz till the herbs have stained the yoghurt green. Set aside in the fridge until you are ready to serve the fish cakes.

To make the fish cakes, mix the spices and water together to make a paste. Heat the oil and gently fry the onion until it is golden, then stir in the spices and fry very gently without burning for a minute. Stir in the garlic and remove from the heat.

Stir the spice mix into the potatoes, and then add the fish and coriander. Season with salt and pepper to taste.

Shape the mixture into eight cakes, dust with flour, dip into the egg and then press into the crumbs. Leave to rest in the fridge for about 30 minutes.

Heat the oil in a large pan, then fry the fish cakes in batches till golden and heated through. Keep warm and when they are all cooked, serve with a salad of chopped cucumber, carrot, tomatoes and green chilli. Serve the minted chilli drizzle on the side.

SERVES 4

Paneer is just my absolute best. If you haven't tried it, it is a soft crumbly-textured cheese used extensively in Indian cuisine for both sweet and savoury dishes. It is not always easy to buy, but it is so easy to make, that you will be cooking with it before you know it. I will always be grateful to Miriam for the hands-on class she gave to me.

Paneer

- 2 litres fresh full cream milk
- 1 cup natural yoghurt
- 2 tsp fresh lemon juice

Place the milk in a large saucepan, bearing in mind that once the milk starts to boil it will rise up. Make sure that it has a heavy base so that the milk doesn't burn.

Okay, now that the milk is in the right pot, bring it to the boil and let it rise to the top. Add the yoghurt and lemon juice and give it a stir to get the milk to curdle. If it takes too long, add another teaspoon of lemon juice. The curds will begin to form and separate from the whey – at this point take the saucepan off the heat.

Have a large sieve ready, lined with muslin or linen cheesecloth, steady it over a large bowl and pour the curds into it. Throw out the whey. Now you need to run some cold water gently through the curds. Pull the cloth up around the cheese and tie it up, then let it drip for 15 minutes.

Now place the cheese (still in the muslin) onto a baking tray. Place a heavy weight on it to press out any liquid – a pot about the same size as the cheese filled with cold water makes a perfect weight and helps to shape the cheese. Leave for an hour. The cheese is now ready to cut.

I like to place the paneer on a plate drizzled liberally with extra virgin olive oil and then topped with any of the following: toasted cumin seeds; red and green sliced chilli; freshly chopped coriander; chopped roasted, salted peanuts; fresh lemon zest; flaked salt; freshly ground black pepper; and always a splash of freshly squeezed lemon juice.

SERVES 4

Saag Paneer

- 5 Tbs peanut oil
- 300 g well-drained paneer, cubed
- 2 Tbs ghee, or unsalted butter
- 1 onion, thinly sliced
- 2 tsp grated ginger
- 2 cloves garlic, grated
- 1 chilli, deseeded and chopped
- 1 tsp cumin
- ½ tsp turmeric
- 2 tomatoes, grated
- 800 g spinach, finely chopped
- salt and pepper
- ¾ cup fresh cream
- garam masala

When Miriam first said that she was going to make saag paneer, I said I wasn't so sure about the 'saag bit of the dish'. She collapsed with laughter and said that it was only a cheese and spinach dish – it was time to learn the Indian names of ingredients.

Heat the oil in a large frying pan and fry the paneer in batches till golden on all sides. Keep to one side.

Heat the ghee in a saucepan and fry the onion, ginger, garlic, chilli, cumin and turmeric together; don't burn it! Cook stirring for seven minutes until golden, then add the tomatoes and cook for five minutes more.

Add the spinach and once it wilts season with salt and pepper. Stir in the cream with a pinch of masala. Return the paneer to the pan and warm through.

Serve with cardamom rice (page 161) or roti (page 146).

SERVES 4

Mrs Brookes, our next-door neighbour, had an Indian housekeeper called Mary and she used to make dal once a week. The smells that drifted over the hedge used to make my mouth ache for what she was cooking, so I took the bull by the horns and asked Mary to show me how to cook it the way she did. So, for a small fee, Mary jumped the fence and joined me at the stove to spill the beans and share her secrets.

She said she made dal for her own family at least three times a week, once with meat and twice without. She said it was really healthy: a good source of protein, and almost fat free. We made it with lamb which Mary said makes it fattening, but my mouth was screaming for a bowl of that yummy stuff served with rice and a delicious topping of fried onions, ginger, garlic, cumin, mustard seeds and dried chillies. That's what makes a hungry woman happy!

Yummy Dal Tadka

THE DAL

- 2 Tbs vegetable oil
- 1 Tbs ghee
- 200 g lamb knuckle
- salt, to taste
- 1½ tsp black mustard seeds
- 1 large onion, finely chopped
- 2 cloves garlic, finely chopped
- 2 tsp chopped fresh ginger
- 1 tsp ground cumin
- 1 tsp ground turmeric
- 1 cardamom pod, split
- 2 green chillies, deseeded and chopped
- 200 g mung dal or red lentils
- 6 cups water or chicken stock
- 1 fresh bay leaf
- fresh coriander

THE TADKA

- 1½ Tbs oil or ghee
- ½ tsp mustard seeds
- 2 dried chillies
- 6 curry leaves
- ¼ tsp fennel seeds
- 1 tsp cumin seeds
- 1 onion, very thinly sliced

Place the oil and ghee into a heavy-based saucepan and heat. Season the lamb and brown it on all sides. Leave it in the saucepan and add the mustard seeds. Let them pop and then add the onion, garlic and ginger, cooking for about five to eight minutes.

Now add the cumin, turmeric, cardamom and chillies, and stir for two minutes, adding a little water if it looks as if it might stick.

Add the lentils, water and bay leaf, and bring to the boil. Cover and simmer for about 40 to 50 minutes. Add a little hot water if needed, season with salt, and stir in some chopped coriander.

While the dal is simmering, prepare the tadka. Heat the oil in a frying pan and add the mustard seeds. Let them pop and then stir in the chillies, curry leaves, fennel and cumin seeds, and cook for a minute. Add the onion and cook till golden brown.

Ladle the dal into a bowl, spoon over the tadka and serve.

SERVES 4

Fried Yoghurt Bread Rounds

- 2 cups flour, sifted
- 2 tsp baking powder
- 1 tsp salt
- 1 tsp sugar
- 1 egg, beaten
- 3 Tbs natural yoghurt
- 1 tsp toasted cumin seeds
- oil for deep frying

These are great to serve with a curry or soup and can be fried just before serving. Mary used to make these sometimes to serve with the dal and would pass a few over the hedge to me.

Place the dry ingredients into a bowl, add the egg and yoghurt and mix together well. You may add a little water, should you need it. Knead for five to eight minutes, cover and let the dough rest for three hours while you get on with other things. (I would have a deep bubble bath at this point!)

Tip the dough out onto a floured surface and knead it for a minute or so and then divide it into 12 balls. Roll them out to 13 cm rounds.

Heat the oil in a deep pan and fry the bread rounds one at a time, pressing them under the oil so that they can puff up. Once they are golden on all sides, remove and drain on paper towels. Serve warm.

MAKES 12

The one thing I learned from Miriam is that a recipe is just a guideline of flavours and combinations of ingredients: dishes are very personal to your own taste; curries are as varied as the people who cook them; and a masala changes from household to household. She taught me that Indian food does not have to be as hot as the breath of the devil; it is about harmony in your mouth, and heat that is comfortable for the individual.

This salad is served nice and chilled with a tandoori-style roast chicken or barbequed meats. It was inspired by all the raitas and sambals that I love served alongside a curry. I just adore the smoky flavour of flame-grilled brinjals, but if you don't have a gas hob you can bake them in the oven.

Bollywood Brinjals and New Potatoes

YOGHURT DRESSING

- 2 cups thick natural yoghurt
- 1 Tbs freshly-squeezed lemon juice
- 1 green chilli, deseeded
- 1 Tbs chopped mint
- 1 Tbs chopped coriander
- 1 clove garlic, crushed
- 1 tsp toasted and ground cumin
- ½ tsp salt

THE SALAD

- 3 large firm brinjals
- 350 g new potatoes, cooked, peeled and halved
- 1 medium red onion, thinly sliced
- 12 large fresh mint leaves, chopped
- 1 cup peeled and chopped cucumber
- fresh coriander sprigs
- salt, to taste

Place the dressing ingredients in a food processor and give it a good whizz, blending well. Taste and adjust the seasoning.

Place the brinjals onto the open flame on your gas hob and keep turning them with a pair of tongs until they are soft all over. Watch them carefully as this happens quickly. Put them in a bowl covered with plastic wrap and leave them to cool.

If you are baking them, place them in an oven preheated to 180 °C. Check them after 15 minutes and cook till softened.

Peel the brinjals and chop them roughly. Keep all the smoky juices to spoon back onto the chopped flesh.

Place the potatoes and brinjals into a bowl with half the onion, the mint, cucumber and coriander. Season with a little salt, pour over the yoghurt dressing and toss lightly.

Assemble the salad on a platter and garnish with the remaining onions and a few sprigs of fresh coriander.

SERVES 6

Bombay Potato and Cauliflower

- 450 g potatoes, peeled and cubed
- 1 tsp turmeric
- 1½ cups cauliflower florets, roughly chopped
- 4 Tbs vegetable oil or ghee
- 2 dried red chillies
- 2 onions, finely chopped
- 2 fresh green chillies, chopped
- 50 g fresh coriander, chopped
- ¼ tsp asafoetida
- 8 curry leaves
- ½ tsp fennel seeds
- ½ tsp cumin seeds
- ½ tsp white mustard seeds
- ½ tsp onion seeds
- ½ tsp nigella seeds
- salt and freshly ground black pepper
- lemon juice
- fresh coriander leaves and stems, chopped, for serving

I love leftovers of this dish topped with a soft poached or fried egg.

Boil the potatoes in salted water with half of the turmeric till just tender. Remove with a slotted spoon and boil the cauliflower for five minutes in the same water. Remove and drain.

Heat the oil or ghee in a frying pan and fry the dried chillies till they start to darken, and then add the onions, green chillies, fresh coriander and remaining turmeric. Stir together well.

Now add the asafoetida, curry leaves, and the fennel, cumin, mustard, onion and nigella seeds. Keep cooking till the onions soften, and give it a few good stirs while it simmers.

Stir in the potatoes and cauliflower with a tablespoon or two of warm water, and cook over a slow heat for 10 minutes. Give it a stir from time to time to coat the vegetables. Season with salt and pepper, and add a squeeze of fresh lemon juice to sharpen the flavour. Stir in the coriander and serve.

SERVES 4

Cardamom and Cumin Scented Rice

- 1½ cups basmati rice
- 2 Tbs ghee or unsalted butter
- 4 split cardamom pods
- 1 tsp cumin seeds
- small piece cinnamon stick
- ¾ tsp black mustard seeds
- 1 tsp salt
- 2 cups water
- extra knob of butter

Wash the rice a few times to clean it and remove some of the starch. Now pre-soak the rice in cold water for 30 minutes before cooking it, drain and set aside.

Heat the ghee or butter in a saucepan large enough to hold the rice once it has cooked, and add the cardamom, cumin, cinnamon and mustard seeds. Stir fry for half a minute, then stir in the rice and coat in the spicy butter. Season with the salt and add the water.

Bring the pot to the boil, cover and turn the heat right down. Don't lift the lid for about nine minutes (you want the rice to steam) and then check that the rice has absorbed all the water.

Remove from the heat, add an extra knob of butter and gently toss with two forks.

SERVES 4 TO 6

The first time I tasted kulfi was at an Indian wedding. I must have been about 13 at the time, and I have never forgotten the texture and flavour. It was like nothing I had ever tasted before and I always wanted to learn how to make it so that I could eat it for the rest of my life.

Mary said that kulfi was always served in her home for special occasions. When she was growing up they never even considered buying commercial ice cream and ever since the day her family got a fridge with a freezer box they made their own.

She put milk into a pot and while it was slowly cooking down, she told me stories about how her family came to be in South Africa from India. As she reminisced, she kept stirring away to stop the milk from sticking to the bottom of the pot. It seemed to take forever for it to thicken up nicely, but nothing would make Mary cheat and just open up a can of evaporated milk. And besides, she said, something this good was worth waiting for. If you want dense and creamy kulfi, you have to be patient. She never lied about that!

Pistachio Kulfi

- 8 cups full cream milk
- 4 Tbs sugar, or to your taste
- ¾ tsp ground toasted green cardamom seeds
- 1 Tbs blanched and skinned, finely ground pistachios
- 1 Tbs rose water
- silver leaf, to garnish (optional)
- rose petals of your choice
- 1½ Tbs blanched and skinned pistachios, thinly sliced

Pour the milk and sugar into a wide-mouthed heavy-bottomed saucepan (the milk will reduce quicker than in a small saucepan) and bring it to the boil over a high heat. Stir constantly.

Okay, now grab a book and settle at the stove. Lower the heat, add the cardamom and cook the milk, stirring constantly, until it has thickened and reduced to about half. Don't scald the milk – it will affect the taste. This takes about 40 to 50 minutes, but trust me, it is worth it!

Once the milk is thick and reduced, stir in the ground pistachio nuts and rose water, and cool the mixture down.

Pour the mixture into kulfi moulds, cocktail bread tins or small ramekins, filling them evenly. Cover with plastic wrap or foil to keep other flavours out, then freeze overnight or until firmly set.

Remove the kulfi from the freezer 10 minutes before you are ready to serve, and then de-mould by running a warm sharp knife around the edges of the ramekins.

Plate each kulfi onto a dessert plate, cut each one into slices, and serve garnished with silver leaf, sugared rose petals and a scattering of chopped pistachios.

TIP: I like to make these the day before I need them so that they set nice and firm. If you would like to try a mango version, replace the rose water and pistachios with 1½ cups fresh mango pulp.

SERVES 6

CHINA

When I was growing up and first tasted westernised Chinese food, I was hardly impressed. The spring rolls were full of hot oil; if you took a bite the person sitting opposite could get oil in the eye. The noodles were soggy, the cheap vinegar made the sweet more sour, and every dish tasted the same. I was put off for life, it would seem.

My perception of Chinese food was changed about 10 years ago when I met Chuck and Tina Yang. In those days they had a small family-run restaurant that seated about 40 people called The Yellow River. It had bright lights and the Formica-topped tables were reserved for the local Chinese community. As I walked in I was already in love with all the delicious aromas that filled the room.

The food smelled beautifully earthy and sweet and the sight of chatty slurping Chinese families made me impatient to scoop a heaped chopstick of sticky steamed gleaming white rice straight into my mouth.

The tables were covered with hotpots and dumplings, whole deep-fried fish, and crispy salt and pepper calamari. I saw some fat, sticky-sweet chilli prawns that I longed to try, and noodles with shredded chilli, ginger, garlic and pork. And then there was tofu, egg, bright green Chinese veggies and sprouts all floating in steaming bowls of chicken broth. And platters of deep-fried soft-shell crab, and succulent chunks of chicken cooked with ginger, heaps of whole dried chillies and fragrant roasted peanuts.

I loved how everyone was sharing the meal from different dishes, everything sliced or chopped to bite-size so that it could just be slipped into the mouth with chopsticks, no cutlery required.

I had walked into a world of flavour, hot and spicy, pungent and salty, sweet and sour, cold and tasty, crisp and soft. My hunger to visit and taste China had begun!

I love visiting Suzhou, which is known as the Venice of China. Half of the city is covered by water and quaint little houses line the canals; it is a sight too beautiful to behold. Sadly the homes don't have plumbing, so the authorities are slowly moving people into apartments and some of this old-world living on the water will be lost.

I am happiest and most inspired when I am surrounded by fresh produce, and that is why I love to visit fresh food markets. At the local market in Suzhou, my heart raced at the sight of unusual ingredients just begging to be turned into dinner: mounds of every kind of fresh mushroom imaginable; snake beans thick and long and so fresh they sounded like a bone breaking when snapped in half; heaps of the longest, juiciest, whitest mung bean sprouts I have ever seen in my life; piles of lean pork cuts, pale pink and fleshy, covered with the smoothest skin waiting to be crackled. I had a meal in my head that needed to be cooked!

Pork Neck with Beans and Sprouts

- 300 g piece of deboned pork neck or fillet
- salt, to taste
- ½ tsp ground white pepper
- 4 Tbs cornflour
- 2 tsp brown sugar
- 3 Tbs soy sauce
- 1 tsp sesame oil
- 1 tsp grated garlic
- 1 tsp grated fresh ginger
- 2 egg whites, gently whipped
- 200 g tender green beans, roughly chopped
- 3 Tbs peanut oil
- 1 heaped Tbs finely chopped ginger
- 1 large red onion, and thinly sliced
- 4 cloves chopped garlic
- 1 fresh or dried chilli, chopped
- 150 g fresh mung bean sprouts
- ¾ cup warm chicken stock
- 4 spring onions with tops, sliced
- handful fresh coriander, chopped

I had the pleasure of cooking this pork dish for the Chef lecturers at the University of Suzhou. The chefs showed off some fine cutting skills – they sliced the pork thinner than a shoelace!

To make slicing the pork easier, place it in the freezer for a little while to firm it up. Now slice it thinly against the grain and then cut the slices as thinly as you can into strips.

Place the sliced pork in a bowl and season with salt and pepper. Stir in the cornflour, brown sugar, soy sauce, sesame oil, garlic, grated ginger and egg whites. Be sure to coat the pork well.

Blanch the green beans for two minutes in boiling water, then set aside.

Heat the oil in a wok or large frying pan and add the chopped ginger and the onion. Fry till the ginger becomes fragrant and the onion softens; about five minutes. Add the garlic, chilli and pork, and stir fry till the pork is almost cooked.

Add the mung beans, chicken stock and green beans, and simmer for five minutes. Stir in the spring onions and coriander, adding a little more stock if needed.

Serve with steamed rice.

SERVES 4

HONEY GINGER DIPPING SAUCE

- ½ cup soy sauce
- 3 Tbs black Chinese vinegar or balsamic
- 1 Tbs finely chopped fresh ginger
- 2 cloves garlic, crushed
- 1 tsp sesame oil
- 1 Tbs vegetable oil
- 2 tsp runny honey
- 1 red chilli, sliced
- 1 spring onion with tops, thinly sliced
- 1 Tbs roughly chopped fresh coriander

DUMPLINGS

- 2 star anise
- 2 cups water
- 10 medium-sized dried shiitake mushrooms
- 450 g freshly minced pork neck
- 200 g chopped raw prawn meat
- ½ cup finely chopped bamboo shoots
- 3 spring onions with tops, finely chopped
- 1 egg white, lightly beaten
- salt, to taste
- 2 tsp light soy sauce
- 2 tsp flour
- ½ tsp sesame oil
- ½ tsp white pepper
- ½ small red chilli, chopped
- 3 Tbs fresh chopped coriander
- 2 tsp chopped garlic
- 40 wonton wrappers

I once had the pleasure and honour of celebrating the Chinese New Year with my agent Ping and her family in Beijing. After an amazing dinner at a fancy hotel restaurant, we made our way to Ping's home to bring the New Year in with handmade dumplings.

Making New Year dumplings in the shape of money bags is a Northern Chinese tradition and is thought to bring wealth to those who eat them. Traditionally, at the stroke of midnight, everyone assembles in the kitchen and rolls dumplings together while the broth bubbles on the stove.

What a fun-filled celebration it was. Most of the family was wearing red – it is believed to be a lucky colour that will ward off any evil spirits lurking about. Wherever you look in China during the New Year festivities you will see red.

Open Top Pork Dumplings

These are delicious served with my honey ginger dipping sauce!

Make the dipping sauce first so that the flavours get a chance to develop. Place all the ingredients into a jar with a tight-fitting lid and give it a good shake. Set aside.

Now make the dumplings. Boil the star anise in the water for a few minutes. Place the mushrooms in a bowl and soak them in the spiced water until they are soft; around 30 minutes.

Take the mushrooms out of the water and discard the hard stem. Rinse and squeeze the moisture from the caps and chop them finely.

Mix the chopped mushrooms with the remaining ingredients and allow them to rest for an hour before filling your wonton wrappers.

Lay the wonton wrappers out a few at a time onto a floured work surface. Cut the corners of the wrappers to make circles. Place a tablespoon of the pork mixture into the centre of each circle. Bring the edges up around the pork filling, leaving the top open. Continue until you have filled all the wontons.

Place the dumplings in a bamboo steaming basket, cover and steam for 20 minutes. Top up with more boiling water if needed. I like to put the mushroom water and star anise into the pot – this makes for delicious steam.

Serve the dumplings hot with some dipping sauce on the side.

SERVES 4 TO 6

We cooked these spare ribs as well as many other dishes at the Culinary Institute in Suzhou. The ribs are cooked twice to get them really nice and crisp; they were a hit with the group and I am sure you will love them too.

Suzhou-style Crispy Fried Pork Spare Ribs

- 1 Tbs grated fresh ginger
- 4 cloves garlic, crushed
- ¾ cup crunchy peanut butter
- ½ cup custard powder
- salt and white pepper
- 2 Tbs soy sauce
- 2 tsp sesame oil
- 2 egg whites, beaten
- 1.5 to 2 kg pork spare ribs, portioned
- oil for deep frying

Mix all the ingredients, except for the ribs and oil, in a large bowl. Add the ribs and coat well.

Heat some oil to deep-fry the ribs in batches. Do not cook them all the way; remove and drain on paper towels.

When they have cooled down, reheat the oil and deep-fry till golden and crispy. Drain and serve straight away.

Serve with Chuckey's Chicken Sauce (see recipe on page 180). Don't forget a finger bowl laced with fresh lemon juice and lots of paper serviettes too!

SERVES 4

Salt and Pepper Calamari

- 1 kg cleaned calamari tubes
- ¾ cup cornflour
- 1 tsp sea salt
- 2 tsp ground white pepper
- 1 tsp ground cumin
- 1 Tbs very finely chopped ginger
- 1 Tbs very finely chopped garlic
- ½ tsp chilli powder
- 2 egg whites, lightly beaten
- 2 Tbs water
- oil for deep frying

Cut the calamari tubes open, flatten them out and scrape clean. Score the flesh in a diagonal pattern with a sharp knife, then cut the calamari into strips.

Place the strips in a glass bowl with the cornflour, salt, pepper, cumin, ginger, garlic, chilli powder, egg whites and water. Mix together well to coat the calamari.

Heat the oil in a large pan and deep-fry the calamari until golden and crispy. Drain on paper towels and serve immediately.

SERVES 4

Chuck Yang, a Chinese chef in Cape Town who cooks me the most delicious food ever, cooks up a similar dish – and this is my take on his calamari.

The Chinese eat a lot of eggs and this version of foo yong is delicious served hot or cold. You can really own this recipe and fill the omelette with any kind of fish or fowl, mushrooms or veggies you choose.

Egg Foo Yong My Way

OMELETTE
- 2 Tbs vegetable or peanut oil
- 1 red onion, sliced
- 3 cloves garlic, crushed and chopped
- 2 cm ginger, finely chopped
- 1 small red pepper, sliced
- 2 spring onions, sliced
- small handful coriander, roughly chopped
- 1 cup mung bean sprouts
- ½ tsp cornflour
- a little sesame oil, to taste
- soy sauce, to taste
- 10 eggs, beaten

GARNISH
- 2 large spring onions with tops, sliced
- fresh coriander, chopped
- 1 red chilli, chopped
- soy sauce
- sesame oil

Heat just over half of the oil in a wok or large non-stick frying pan and gently fry the onion, garlic and ginger until soft and fragrant. Add the peppers and spring onions, and stir fry for two minutes. Stir in the coriander, mung beans and cornflour, and flavour with some sesame oil and soy sauce. Cook for two minutes, stirring.

Remove from the heat, spoon into a bowl and set aside.

Heat the remaining oil in the same wok and pour in the beaten egg. Swirl the egg from side to side in the wok, then using a spatula pull the egg away from the sides so that the uncooked egg can flow to the bottom of the wok.

Once the edges are firm and the middle only slightly undercooked, spoon the stir fry in the centre of the omelette and spread it out.

Gently lift half of the omelette, fold it on top of itself and press it down flat. Place a plate over the wok and tip the omelette out. Be careful not to overcook the egg, as it continues to steam once it has been inverted onto the plate.

Garnish the top with the sliced spring onions, fresh coriander and chilli, and drizzle over a little soy sauce and sesame oil.

TIP: Make sure the eggs are fresh before you use them. Place them in a bowl of cold water – if they float, turf them out.

SERVES 4 TO 6

Taking my mouth on a tasting spree in China I discovered a whole new world of wonderful textures and flavours; I found that spring onions, garlic and ginger were used in most of the dishes I tried.

Pork and Prawn Egg Rolls

STUFFING
- 2 Tbs vegetable oil
- 2 cloves garlic, crushed
- 1 tsp grated fresh ginger
- 1 tsp crushed dried chillies
- 2 spring onions with tops, finely chopped
- 200 g pork mince
- 150 g raw prawn meat, chopped
- 1 small carrot, finely diced
- 200 g fresh bean sprouts
- 1 tsp sesame oil
- 1 Tbs soy sauce
- ½ tsp salt
- ½ tsp white sugar
- ½ tsp ground white pepper
- 1 Tbs chopped mint
- 1 Tbs coriander

BATTER
- 75 g sifted cake flour
- 1¼ cups cold water
- 6 eggs, beaten
- oil for deep frying

Gently heat the oil in a large frying pan and add the garlic, ginger, chillies and spring onions. Cook for three minutes, stirring.

Mix the pork mince and chopped prawns together, and stir into the spring onion mix. Cook stirring for five minutes. Add the diced carrot, sprouts, sesame oil, soy sauce, salt, sugar and white pepper, and cook till the sprouts start to soften.

Stir in the mint and coriander and remove from the heat.

Place the batter ingredients into a bowl and whisk together until smooth. Oil a small (20 cm) heavy-based frying pan and heat it. Spoon enough batter into the pan to make a thin pancake and cook it on one side. Slide it from the pan onto a plate.

Continue to make more pancakes in this way until all the batter has been used up.

Lay the pancakes out, cooked side up, onto a clean flat surface. Divide the filling amongst the pancakes, placing a portion of the filling in the centre of each one. Fold the nearest edge of the pancake over the filling, fold both sides in towards the centre and then roll up nice and tight. Wet the last edge with water or soy sauce and seal the roll.

Heat the oil in a large frying pan to 180 °C and fry the rolls a few at a time till golden and crisp. Drain on paper towels.

Serve hot with soy sauce or sweet chilli sauce.

SERVES 4

Walnuts

- ¾ cup runny honey
- 3 tsp soy sauce
- 1 tsp sesame oil
- ½ tsp Chinese five-spice powder (optional)
- 2 tsp freshly squeezed lemon juice
- 300 g shelled walnuts
- enough castor sugar to coat
- oil for shallow frying

These appear on a Chinese dining table at any time during the meal. Their gorgeous sweet-salty flavour and their crunchy texture are quiet addictive; it is very hard to restrain yourself from scooping them up in yours hands. That would definitely not be considered good manners and would most certainly offend the host, so you daintily take a few with your chopsticks – but trust me, a few are never enough!

Mix together the honey, soy sauce, sesame oil, five-spice powder and lemon juice. Now stir in the nuts and let them marinate for two hours, giving them a stir every so often.

Remove the nuts from the marinade and coat them in castor sugar. Heat just enough oil to cover the nuts in a large frying pan and cook them until they are nice and golden. Drain on paper towels and enjoy!

Beef and Noodle Stir Fry

BEEF STRIPS

- 200 g sirloin, sliced very thinly and cut into strips
- 4 garlic cloves, crushed
- ½ red chilli, chopped (optional)
- 1½ Tbs cornflour
- 1 egg white, lightly beaten

NOODLE STIR FRY

- peanut oil, for frying
- dried chillies, to taste
- 1 thumb ginger, sliced into matchsticks
- 1 red onion, thinly sliced
- 2 leeks, thinly sliced
- 3 cloves garlic, crushed
- 2 red peppers, thinly sliced
- 1 yellow pepper, thinly sliced
- 100 g white button mushrooms, cut in half
- 3 baby marrows, cut into matchsticks
- 2½ Tbs palm sugar
- ⅓ cup Indonesian soy sauce
- 2 bricks egg noodles, soaked for 10 minutes in warm water
- 5 spring onions, thinly sliced
- 2 Tbs sesame seeds, toasted
- handful mint, chopped
- handful basil, ripped
- 2 Tbs soy sauce, or to taste
- 1 tsp sesame oil, or to taste

Start off by mixing together the beef strips, garlic, chilli, cornflour and egg white in a bowl. If the beef strips cling together too much, add another egg white to loosen them. Set aside.

Now, make the stir fry. Heat the oil in a wok and add the dried chillies to infuse the oil. Remove the chillies when they start to darken, and add the ginger. Fry for a few seconds, then add the onion and fry until it becomes translucent. Add the leeks and garlic. Toss for a few seconds and then add the peppers, mushrooms and baby marrows, and stir fry for four minutes. Remove from the wok and set aside.

Add more oil to the wok if necessary and start frying the beef very quickly in batches, taking each batch out once it's done. Take care not to overcook the beef – rather undercook it as it will continue cooking when you take it out of the wok.

Keeping the last batch in the wok, add the palm sugar and stir until the sugar has melted. Add the remaining beef and cooked stir fry, along with the Indonesian soy sauce, and toss with two wooden spoons.

Add the soaked noodles, spring onion, sesame seeds and herbs. Toss through gently, taking care not to over-mix the stir fry.

Add the soy sauce and sesame oil and adjust the seasoning to taste. Serve immediately.

SERVES 4 TO 6

Celery and Peanut Salad

- 2 Tbs soy sauce
- 2 tsp brown sugar
- salt, to taste
- 1 tsp grated fresh ginger
- 2 cloves garlic, crushed
- ¾ tsp sesame oil
- 6 large trimmed celery sticks
- ¾ cup raw peanuts, roasted
- ½ cup chopped fresh coriander
- 1 Tbs toasted sesame seeds

Mix together the soy sauce, sugar, salt, ginger, garlic and sesame oil.

Slice the celery into bite-sized pieces. Blanch in boiling water and let it stand for a minute. Drain, place in a bowl and stir in the dressing, peanuts and coriander.

Chill till you want to serve it, then spoon onto a serving plate and scatter with the toasted sesame seeds.

SERVES 4

Sweet and Sour Cucumber

- 2 firm, very fresh English cucumbers
- salt
- 2 Tbs sugar
- ¼ tsp ground white pepper
- 3 Tbs white wine vinegar
- 1 Tbs sesame oil
- 3 Tbs peanut oil
- 3 cloves garlic, thinly sliced
- 2 cm ginger, thinly sliced and cut into matchsticks
- 1 large red chilli, thinly sliced (optional)

Top and tail the cucumber and slice in half lengthways. Cut into short batons and sprinkle with salt. Leave to sweat for about 10 minutes or so.

Shake together the remaining ingredients in a glass jar with a tight lid. Drain the cucumber and place it in a shallow bowl. Throw on the sweet and sour dressing, toss to coat and chill the salad for a few hours.

Arrange the cucumber batons on a serving plate, spoon over the dressing and serve.

SERVES 6

Deep-fried Beans

- 500 g fresh young green beans, trimmed
- 3 cloves garlic, finely chopped
- 2 tsp very finely chopped ginger
- 1 Tbs black beans, chopped (optional)
- 4 Tbs cornflour
- 2 egg whites, lightly beaten
- salt and white pepper
- 1 tsp sesame oil
- 1 Tbs soy sauce
- oil for deep frying

These beans are so very yummy I could eat piles of them at one sitting. They are inspired by a dish I had once in China.

Cut the beans in half. Mix together the garlic, ginger, black beans, cornflour, egg whites, salt, pepper, sesame oil and soy sauce in a shallow bowl. Add the green beans and toss them well to coat.

Heat the oil in a large frying pan and fry the beans until crisp and golden. Serve with a splash of soy sauce or just as they are.

SERVES 4

Basic Egg-fried Rice

- 4 Tbs oil, for stir frying
- 2 spring onions with tops, cut at an angle
- 3 extra-large eggs, beaten
- 4 cups cold, very dry precooked rice
- 1–2 Tbs light soy sauce
- salt and ground white pepper, to taste

Chuck told me that the secret to eggfried rice is to have the rice cooked, very dry and cold before frying it.

Heat a wok or frying pan and then add two tablespoons of oil to it. Once the oil is hot, stir fry the spring onions lightly for a few seconds. Then pour in the beaten eggs and cook them, stirring all the time until they are very lightly scrambled. Don't cook them dry. Transfer to a bowl and clean the wok.

Add the remaining two tablespoons of oil to the wok and heat it. Add the rice and stir fry for a few minutes, using chopsticks to break it apart (a spoon will break the rice). Stir in the soy sauce and heat the rice through.

Stir in the eggs and spring onions, season to taste, heat through and serve.

SERVES 4 TO 6

This is for my wonderful, loveable friend Chuck Yang, his wife Tina, and his children Jessica and Aaron. He cooks a similar dish at his new restaurant, Chuck Yang's Speciality Dish. He serves it on fragrant sticky egg-fried rice (see recipe on page 179).

CHUCKEY'S SAUCE
- 1 Tbs oil
- 3 Tbs finely chopped fresh ginger
- 4 cloves garlic, chopped
- 2 whole star anise pods
- ½ cup brown sugar
- 2 Tbs soy sauce
- ¾ cup water
- 2 Tbs tomato purée
- 1 Tbs red wine vinegar
- ½ tsp English mustard powder
- ½ cup teriyaki sauce
- 2 Tbs hoisin sauce
- ¼ tsp sesame oil

THE CHICKEN
- 6 chicken breasts, sliced into strips crossways
- 1 Tbs grated ginger
- 2 cloves garlic, finely chopped
- 1 Tbs soy sauce
- a good shake of ground white pepper
- a grinding of Sichuan pepper (optional)
- 1 green chilli, finely chopped
- 5 Tbs cornflour
- 2 egg whites, beaten
- oil for deep frying

TO FINISH
- 1 Tbs oil
- 2 red chillies, chopped
- 2 cloves garlic, chopped
- 4 spring onions with tops, chopped
- ½ cup roughly chopped fresh coriander

Chuckey's Chinese Chicken

Make the sauce first. Heat the oil gently and cook the ginger, garlic and star anise for a minute. Stir in the sugar, soy sauce, water, tomato purée, vinegar, mustard and teriyaki sauce, and cook simmering till the sugar has melted. Add the hoisin sauce and cook for five minutes. Add the sesame oil and remove from the heat. Set aside until needed.

Place the chicken in a bowl with the ginger, garlic, soy sauce, white pepper, Sichuan pepper and chilli. Use your clean hands to mix everything together well, and then stir in the cornflour and egg whites, coating the chicken with it. Leave to marinate for 30 minutes.

Heat the oil in a wok and fry the chicken in small batches till golden and crisp but not cooked through.

To finish the dish, heat a tablespoon of oil in a large frying pan, add the chillies, garlic and two of the spring onions and fry for three minutes, stirring. Add the reserved sauce and bring to the boil. Toss the chicken into the sauce and stir to coat.

Stir in the remaining spring onions and coriander, and serve with sticky rice and extra soy sauce.

TIP: The seeds of the star anise have a delicious aniseed flavour. It is a beautiful, woody, star-shaped pod and I always leave it in the food as a garnish.

SERVES 4 TO 6

Shimeji mushrooms are available quite often these days. When you come across them, please try them. I have had them raw in a salad but I have to say that I found them to be a little bitter. I far prefer them when the heat gets to them – it releases their lovely nutty flavour, and also makes them a lot easier to digest. The whole mushroom is edible; you just have to nip off the tough bit at the bottom. They have a gorgeous meaty texture and are very tasty. Just love them!

Mushroom Chicken Stir Fry

- 6 deboned skinless chicken thighs, cut into bite-sized pieces
- 3 Tbs cornflour
- ½ tsp ground white pepper
- ½ tsp salt
- 1 tsp ground cumin
- 1 Tbs peanut or vegetable oil
- 300 g oyster or shimeji mushrooms
- 6 spring onions with tops, roughly chopped
- 4 cm fresh ginger, cut into very thin matchsticks
- 3 cloves garlic, crushed
- 1 red chilli, thinly sliced
- 1 Tbs oyster sauce
- 2 tsp soy sauce
- 1 Tbs runny honey
- ½ cup vegetable or chicken stock
- ½ cup chopped coriander

Place the chicken into a glass bowl with the cornflour, white pepper, salt and cumin, and mix together to coat.

Heat the oil in a large wok or frying pan and stir fry the chicken in two batches for five minutes. Return all the chicken to the wok and add the mushrooms, spring onions, ginger, garlic and chilli. Cook for a minute, stirring.

Add the oyster and soy sauce and stir well to combine. Add the honey and stock, and cook the chicken till done; about another 10 minutes.

Stir in the coriander and serve with steamed rice or veggie noodles.

SERVES 4

Black Bean Chicken

CHICKEN
- 6 chicken breasts, sliced into bite-sized pieces
- 4 cloves garlic, crushed
- 1 red chilli, chopped
- 4 tsp soy sauce
- ½ tsp sesame oil
- 4 Tbs cornflour

BLACK BEAN STIR FRY
- peanut oil, for frying
- dried chillies, to taste
- 1 thumb ginger, sliced into matchsticks
- 1 red onion, thinly sliced
- ½ cup black beans, finely chopped
- 2 medium leeks, thinly sliced
- 3 cloves garlic, crushed
- 2 red peppers, thinly sliced
- 1 yellow pepper, thinly sliced
- ¾ cup honey
- 2 Tbs soy sauce, or to taste
- 1–2 tsp sesame oil, or to taste
- 5 spring onions, thinly sliced
- handful coriander, chopped
- 2 Tbs sesame seeds, toasted

Black beans are usually available at all Chinese supermarkets, but if you don't manage to find the whole beans you can use five tablespoons of black bean sauce instead.

Place the chicken pieces, garlic, chilli, soy sauce, sesame oil and cornflour in a bowl. Stir well, making sure the chicken is well coated with the cornflour – add a little more, if necessary.

To make the stir fry, heat the oil in a wok and add the chillies to infuse the oil. Remove the chillies when they start to darken and add the ginger. Fry for a few seconds, then add the onion and black beans. Fry until the onion becomes translucent.

Add the leeks and garlic. Toss for a few seconds, and then add the peppers. Drizzle with the honey, soy sauce and sesame oil and remove from the wok to use later.

In the same wok, add a little more oil if necessary and start frying the chicken in batches, removing each batch when crisp and golden. Keep the last batch in the wok when done, return the rest of the chicken to the wok and stir fry.

Toss using two wooden spoons, add the reserved vegetable stir fry and the spring onions. Adjust the seasoning to taste. Add the coriander, sprinkle with toasted sesame seeds and serve immediately with egg-fried rice (see recipe on page 179).

TIP: If you are fond of chilli, like I am, you can add more while you are frying the onions.

SERVES 4

I went into a very upmarket Chinese department store just before the Chinese New Year to purchase something sweet for my guide's family for the New Year. There was a sweet section like nothing I have ever seen before in my life. It was not just a few counters; it was the size of a warehouse. There was every type of dried fruit arranged like works of art, and chocolates, biscuits and sweets in the most exquisite wrappings. But it was the nut and seed brittles that got my blood racing!

Sesame Bars

- 2 cups sugar
- ⅓ cup vinegar
- 1 Tbs warm water
- 75 g sesame seeds, toasted
- 100 g pumpkin seeds, toasted
- 100 g sunflower seeds, toasted

Place the sugar, vinegar and water in a saucepan and stir it until the sugar has dissolved completely. Don't let it burn because it will taste really nasty and you will just have to start again!

Now you need to bring this to the boil but it is important that you do not stir this time; you need to boil it for about 10 minutes until it is nice and golden or has reached the hard crack stage. If you have a sugar thermometer, it should measure 154 °C.

You might as well multi-task while the toffee is bubbling away. Using vegetable oil or non-stick cooking spray, grease a baking tin measuring 18 cm by 28 cm.

Mix the seeds and scatter half of them over the base of the baking tin. Pour the hot toffee over the seeds and using a metal soup ladle with a well-oiled base, smooth the toffee and press it down so that the mixture fills the baking tray.

Scatter the remaining seeds evenly over the toffee, and press them gently down.

Let the toffee cool down a little, but not completely, and using an oiled metal knife cut the toffee into fingers, squares or bars. Separate the bars and allow them to harden completely on waxed paper. Store in an airtight container.

MAKES ABOUT 30 BARS

Bow Ties

THE DOUGH
- 225 g sifted flour
- pinch of salt
- 50 g cold butter, grated
- iced water
- cornflour
- fresh vegetable oil for deep frying

THE SYRUP
- 1 cup golden syrup
- ½ cup runny honey
- 2 Tbs hot water
- 3 Tbs freshly squeezed lemon juice
- 2 cm peeled fresh ginger, bashed
- ½ tsp ground ginger
- ½ cup toasted walnuts, finely chopped
- 2 Tbs toasted sesame seeds

This traditional Chinese dessert is very moreish!

Place the flour and salt in a bowl and, using a metal knife, cut the butter into the flour till it looks crumbly. Make a well in the centre of the mixture and add some iced water, a little at a time. Keep cutting in with the knife, adding little splashes of water as you go to form a smooth firm dough.

Cover the dough in plastic wrap and let it relax for 60 minutes in a cool place. While the dough is resting, make the syrup.

Place the golden syrup, honey, water, lemon juice and ginger into a medium-sized saucepan and bring to the boil. Remove from the heat immediately and set aside. Mix the nuts and sesame seeds together and put them aside for sprinkling on the bow ties once they have been cooked.

Dust a flat surface with cornflour and roll the dough out into a rectangle as thinly as you can. Tidy and trim the edges of the dough and then measure out little rectangles about 10 cm by 5 cm. Pinch and twist the centre of each strip into the shape of bow ties. Continue till they are all done, and chill in the fridge while you heat the oil for deep frying.

Heat the oil in a large pan and deep fry the bow ties a few at a time. Get someone to work alongside you, dipping them into the syrup and shaking off any excess. Place them on a cooling rack over an oven tray to catch any drips, and sprinkle lightly with the nut mix. Serve immediately.

MAKES ABOUT 50

This refreshingly light almond-flavoured syrup with cubes of jelly and fresh fruit was inspired by my dear friend, Chuck Yang. The Chinese often use tinned fruit cocktail, but I love to use soft ripe raspberries when they are available. It is served ice cold.

Chinese Fruit Soup

JELLY CUBES
- 1 can condensed milk
- 3 cups hot water
- 4 tsp powdered gelatine
- 1 Tbs sugar
- 1 tsp almond essence

LIGHT SUGAR SYRUP
- 3 cups water
- 1 cup sugar
- 1 tsp almond essence
- fresh fruits
- lots of ice

Heat the condensed milk and water together gently in a saucepan. Stir to dissolve the condensed milk, but do not allow it to come to the boil. Remove it from the heat.

Mix together the gelatine and sugar, and slowly stir it into the heated liquid. Keep stirring till the gelatine has dissolved. Stir in the almond essence, pour into a shallow square dish and chill till set.

To make the syrup, heat together the water and sugar, stirring until the sugar has dissolved. Cook for five minutes on low with the lid off. Add the almond essence and remove from the heat. Cool before placing the syrup in the fridge to get icy cold.

When you are ready to put it together, place the fruit in a large clear glass serving bowl and add some ice cubes and the sugar syrup. Using clean hands, place them in front of you, open the fingers wide, and gently put those hands into the bowl and give the fruit and syrup a light toss. Hands out, lick them and then give them a good wash.

Take the jelly out of the fridge and cut into bite-sized cubes. Scatter onto the soup and give the bowl a light shake to cover the jelly with the syrup.

If you like the flavour of almond, you can add a little more essence. But take care – it has a strong flavour and can numb your taste buds so that you won't taste anything else.

TIP: Use whatever fresh fruit tickles your fancy – such as watermelon cubes, fresh strawberries halved lengthways, fresh pitted cherries, melon balls, grapes, raspberries or blueberries.

SERVES 6 TO 8

THAILAND

Wonderful friendly fragrant Thailand! I am in love with all things Thai. My experience of the Thai people is that they are very warm and sociable … and always hungry. That's why you will find little food stalls on every street selling delicious fresh food. What I love about eating the Thai way is that there is no such thing as a starter or main, nor is there one dish per person; the food is shared by everyone and that means that the more people there are at the table, the more delicious dishes are served. I am told that the Thai people believe that eating alone is bad luck, so the more the merrier.

One of the things I look forward to when I go to Thailand is a *som tam* salad, a beautiful hot and sour green papaya salad that you can also make from green mangoes. I grow papaya in my garden at home. They hardly ever see the light of day, and when those plump little bodies are still grass green, I shred them into a salad. I pound up some gorgeous fresh lime, chillies – lots of chillies! – fish sauce, palm sugar and garlic. It's one of the most delicious things I've ever tasted.

When I was in Thailand to film a cooking insert for an episode of a television show called *Life's a Journey*, we went to a neighbourhood floating market – not the big tourist one, but the one where the locals shop and eat. There were tables lining the walkway, laden with delicious food – moist, falling-off-the-bone succulent roast pork, with a whole pig's back of crackling; endless desserts; tons of exotic fresh fruit and vegetables; and the Thai version of bouquet garni, fresh bunches of all the right herbs you would need for a dish.

I got to do the one thing I always want to do in a foreign country: buy the ingredients and cook them. Oh, what fun I had!

Satay, which is delicious marinated meat, fish or tofu on a skewer, originated in Java and is cooked over a wood or charcoal fire, then served with various spicy seasonings, sauces and dips. I have eaten it as street food in Malaysia, Singapore, Brunei and Thailand, and I am happy to say that it has spread to my part of the world too. My favourite one here at home is the chicken satay at Wang Thai restaurant. It's the unbelievable sauce that blows my hair back. Oh mama, how yum is that peanut sauce?

Thai Chicken Satay with Two Sauces

Yummy to pluck the succulent chicken pieces off the stick and double-dip into these gorgeous sauces!

CHICKEN SATAY

- 1 kg chicken breast fillets
- ½ tsp ground coriander
- ¼ tsp ground white pepper
- ½ tsp ground turmeric
- 2 tsp grated fresh ginger
- ½ tsp red curry paste
- 2 stems lemon grass, white part only, finely chopped
- 1 tsp salt
- 4 cloves garlic
- 1 Tbs sugar
- ¾ × 400 g can coconut milk

CUCUMBER SAUCE

- 1 cup hot water
- 6 Tbs sugar
- ½ cup rice wine vinegar, or white wine vinegar
- 1 tsp salt
- 1 spring onion with tops, thinly sliced
- 1 cup diced cucumber
- 2 red chillies, thinly sliced into rings
- 1 tsp finely chopped fresh coriander

PEANUT SAUCE

- 2 Tbs oil
- 2 Tbs red curry paste
- 1 stem lemon grass, tender white part only, chopped
- 1 × 400 g can coconut milk
- 4 Tbs crunchy peanut butter
- 4 Tbs palm or brown sugar
- 2 tsp fish sauce
- juice of 1 lime
- salt, to taste

Cut the chicken breast fillets into thin slices and place in a large, flat dish. Place the remaining satay ingredients in a blender and blitz till smooth. Pour over the chicken pieces and marinate for two hours.

Soak some wooden satay sticks in water while the chicken is marinating; this stops them from burning during grilling.

Thread the chicken pieces onto the skewers and grill them over the barbeque or in a hot skillet. Serve hot with the two sauces.

To make the cucumber sauce, place the water into a small saucepan and bring it to the boil. Stir in the sugar and keep stirring until it dissolves, then stir in the vinegar and salt. Remove from the heat and cool. Stir in the spring onion, cucumber, chillies and coriander, and serve.

To make the peanut sauce, heat the oil and stir fry the curry paste and lemon grass for 30 seconds. Add the coconut milk, peanut butter and sugar, and cook till the sauce thickens. Remove from the heat and stir in the fish sauce and lime juice. Taste and season with salt, adjusting the seasoning to suit your taste buds.

SERVES 4 TO 6

We went to the Blue Elephant Bangkok, which is a Thai institution of 30 years' standing, specialising in Royal Thai cuisine. The restaurant is in an historic building surrounded by lush orchid gardens with trickling fountains.

I was very excited to meet the celebrated chef, Khun Nooror Somany Steppe; she and her husband own the Blue Elephant restaurant chain and cooking school worldwide. We filmed together and she did a very traditional Thai dish and I took the Thai ingredients and made something with a twist, a seared tuna with mushrooms.

The name 'Blue Elephant' is taken from the royal colour of the Thai flag and the country's national animal. It is said that if you see an elephant, you'll never forget – because an elephant never forgets. I think that's lovely.

Blue Elephant's Green Papaya Salad with Rainbow Trout

- 2 cloves garlic, peeled
- 5 green bird's eye chillies
- 1 Tbs dried shrimps
- 15 g long French beans, cut into 2 cm pieces
- ½ Tbs palm sugar
- 1½ Tbs fish sauce
- 1½ Tbs lime juice
- 1 tsp tamarind juice
- 35 g cherry tomatoes, cut in half
- 80 g unripe green papaya, peeled and grated into long, thin strips
- 1 Tbs roasted peanuts
- 60 g rainbow trout

In a mortar, roughly pound the garlic and chillies. Add the dried shrimps and pound until crushed. Then add the beans and pound some more.

Add the sugar, fish sauce, lime juice and tamarind juice, and stir together well. Add the tomatoes and press with the pestle.

Add the papaya and peanuts, and stir mixing in well. Transfer to a serving dish and top with slivers of rainbow trout.

MAKES 1 SERVING

Red Prawn Curry

RED CURRY PASTE
- 12 fresh large red chillies, deseeded
- 1 large red onion, chopped
- 5 cloves garlic, peeled
- 4 stalks lemon grass, soft part only, sliced and bruised
- 2 cm ginger, chopped
- 12 coriander stems
- 2 tsp peanut oil
- 2 tsp lime zest
- 2 tsp shrimp paste
- 1 Tbs toasted cumin seeds
- 1 Tbs toasted coriander seeds
- 1 Tbs salt
- 3 fresh or 4 dried lime leaves

PRAWN CURRY
- 1 Tbs sunflower oil
- 1 onion, finely chopped
- 3 cloves garlic, finely chopped
- 1 Tbs finely chopped ginger
- 1 stalk lemon grass, soft part only, finely chopped
- 2 tsp red Thai curry paste
- 1 tsp brown sugar
- 1 × 400 g can chopped tomatoes
- 1 × 400 g coconut milk
- 1 tsp fish sauce
- salt and freshly ground black pepper
- 1 kg cleaned prawns, with head and shell on
- fresh basil, chopped
- fresh coriander, chopped
- zest and juice of 1 lime

Blend all the curry paste ingredients together and liquidise until smooth, adding a little warm water if the paste needs it. You can store whatever you don't use in a clean screw-top jar in the fridge for two weeks, or freeze in portions for three months.

To make the curry, heat the oil in a saucepan and add the onion, garlic, ginger, lemon grass and curry paste. Cook stirring till the fragrance wafts from the saucepan; add a few teaspoons of water if it looks like it is sticking.

Stir in the brown sugar, tomatoes, coconut milk and fish sauce, and cook very gently for six to eight minutes. Season to taste.

Drop the prawns into the sauce a few at a time, simmer gently for 10 minutes, and stir in the basil, coriander, lime zest and juice. Serve with sticky rice.

SERVES 4

It's a common misconception that Thai cuisine is all fiery and hot, but it's not. It's a mixture of flavours – hot, sweet, sour and salty – all balanced, all complementary.

HOT PEANUT SAUCE
- 3 Tbs oil
- 1 small onion, finely diced
- 1 Tbs chopped fresh ginger
- 2 cloves garlic, crushed
- 2 red chillies, chopped
- 1 stalk lemon grass, soft part only, chopped
- 2 tsp tamarind pulp
- 2 Tbs hot water
- ½ cup chunky peanut butter
- ¾ × 400 g can coconut milk
- 1 Tbs palm or brown sugar
- salt, to taste
- 1 Tbs chopped coriander

Heat the oil in a small saucepan and cook the onion, ginger, garlic, chillies and lemon grass till fragrant. Mix the tamarind pulp with the hot water and mash it up, and strain into the saucepan. Add the peanut butter, coconut milk, palm sugar and salt, and simmer gently till the sauce thickens.

Remove from the heat, stir in the coriander and serve with beef, chicken or pork satay. It is glorious drizzled onto steamed rice and makes a great snack when served as a dip for raw vegetables.

LIME DRESSING
- juice of 3 fresh limes
- zest of 2 limes
- 2 tsp brown sugar
- 1 Tbs fish sauce
- ½ cup chopped mint
- ½ cup chopped coriander
- 1 tsp sesame oil
- 1 Tbs peanut oil
- salt and freshly ground black pepper

Shake all the ingredients together in a jar and season to taste. Delicious served with all types of satay and great for fish. It makes a wonderful dressing for a shredded chicken, carrot and cucumber salad.

SWEET CHILLI SYRUP
½ cup rice vinegar
½ cup white sugar
½ cup water
1 Tbs thinly sliced ginger
3 red chillies, sliced
2 cloves garlic, thinly sliced

Place all the ingredients together in a saucepan and boil till reduced by a third. This should be not too thick. If it is reducing too fast, turn down the heat and add a little more rice vinegar. Cool and store till needed. I like to serve it with grilled meats, fish (especially fish cakes), prawns and calamari.

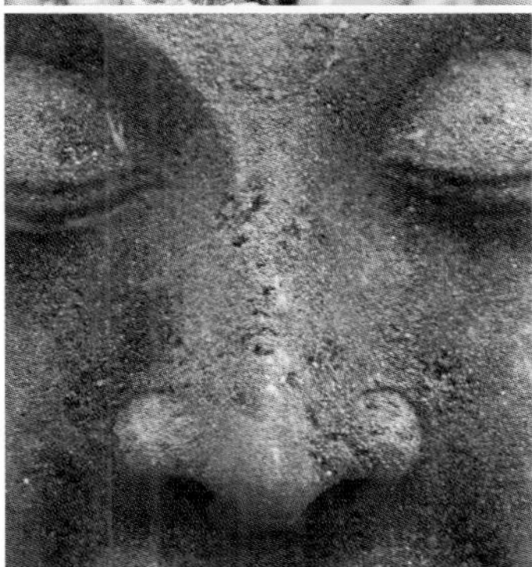

I always think of Thailand as the land of the hairy nut, the coconut. I love everything about it: its flavour, the flesh, the cream, the milk, the water. When I was in the markets, it was amazing to see how they use every part of the coconut: the husk is used for making mattresses; the shell is used by craftsmen; the nut is reduced to cream, and then to milk; and they save the water.

Wok-cooked Fragrant Mussels

- 2 Tbs peanut or olive oil
- 1 tsp green curry paste
- 3 sticks lemon grass, tender inner part, finely chopped
- 3 slices fresh root ginger, bashed
- 2 red chillies, deseeded and sliced
- 2 cloves garlic, chopped
- 3 spring onions with tops, roughly chopped
- 1 × 400 g can coconut milk
- juice and zest of 3 limes
- 1 Tbs fish sauce
- palm sugar or brown sugar, to taste
- 1 Tbs sesame oil
- salt and black pepper
- 2 kg cleaned fresh or frozen mussels
- ½ cup fresh torn basil
- small handful coriander, chopped

The secret is not to overcook these selenium-rich little bodies in a shell; they should be tender, succulent and moist. If you are using frozen mussels, add them at the last moment. Frozen mussels are usually precooked and will become tough and chewy if cooked for too long.

Place the oil in a large, very hot wok or saucepan and add the green curry paste, lemon grass, ginger and chillies, and stir fry for a minute or so till fragrant. Do not burn; add a few drops of water if needed.

Stir in the garlic and spring onions, and fry for 30 seconds. Add the coconut milk, half the lime juice and zest, and the fish sauce. Simmer for three minutes, taste and add the sugar, sesame oil and salt and pepper.

Bring to the boil and then add the mussels and let them simmer gently; give the pot a little shake every so often. Once all the mussels have opened, stir in the basil and coriander. (Be sure to throw away any mussels that remain closed. I mean it, turf any closed mussels away, okay!)

Spoon the mussels into a bowl, give them a splash of the remaining lime juice and a scattering of lime zest, and serve immediately.

SERVES 6

Stuffed Thai Omelettes

PRAWN PORK FILLING
- 2 Tbs olive or vegetable oil
- 1 Tbs finely chopped fresh ginger
- 3 cloves garlic, chopped
- 1 chilli, finely chopped
- 150 g pork neck, finely chopped
- 3 spring onions, finely chopped
- 1 tsp brown sugar
- 1 Tbs soy sauce
- salt and pepper
- 2 stalks lemon grass, inner tender parts, finely chopped
- 150 g prawn meat, finely chopped
- 2 Tbs chopped fresh mint
- 2 Tbs chopped fresh coriander

OMELETTES
- 6 eggs, beaten
- ¾ × 400 g can coconut milk
- 1 Tbs cornflour
- ½ cup chopped coriander
- 3 spring onions with tops, thinly sliced
- 1 small red chilli, diced
- 1 tsp fish sauce
- ½ tsp sesame oil
- oil, for frying

FOR SERVING
- ½ cucumber, deseeded and diced
- 200 g butter lettuce, torn into bite-sized pieces

Make the filling first. Heat the oil and then add the ginger, garlic, chilli and pork and stir well, frying for three minutes. Add the spring onions, brown sugar and soy sauce and fry for a further five minutes. Taste, season with salt and pepper, and stir in the lemon grass.

Stir in the prawns, mint and coriander and cook till the prawns turn pink. Remove from the heat and spoon into a serving bowl.

Place all the omelette ingredients in a bowl and mix well. Heat a little oil in a small frying pan and make a thin omelette. Slide it onto a warm plate, and then make another one. Keep going till the mixture is used up.

To serve, place the omelettes, pork mix, cucumber and lettuce on the table and let everyone fill and roll their own omelettes. Drizzle with sweet chilli syrup (see page 195) or any other sauce you like.

SERVES 4 TO 6

When I smell the kaffir lime leaves – except we're not saying that anymore, it's called *bai makrut* – bubbling in a coconut broth, my juices start flowing, my tummy starts rumbling and I overeat, going from one vendor to the next. I want to try everything the street has to offer. I think I've eaten more meals on the streets of Thailand than I have in their restaurants. Thailand is one of the safest and cleanest countries in the world to eat street food. It's bought fresh in small amounts and is replenished throughout the day. Dishes subtly flavoured with lemon grass and galangal entice me from every stall. It's a feast for the senses.

Coconut Soup with Chicken and Prawns

- 1 cup chicken stock
- 1½ × 400 g cans coconut milk
- 2 thin slices fresh young ginger
- 2 stalks lemon grass, tender inner part only, pounded
- 4 fresh or dried lime leaves, torn
- 1 tsp green curry paste
- 250 g chicken breast fillet, thinly sliced
- 1 Tbs palm sugar or white sugar
- 200 g prawn meat
- 100 g thinly sliced button mushrooms
- 4 Tbs fish sauce
- ½ cup fresh lime juice
- fresh coriander, for garnishing
- sliced green and red chillies (optional) for garnishing

Place the chicken stock and half the coconut milk into a saucepan with the ginger, lemon grass, lime leaves and curry paste, and bring to the boil.

Once it is boiling, add the chicken and palm sugar and simmer for three minutes. Add the rest of the coconut milk, along with the prawns, mushrooms and fish sauce, and bring to the boil.

When the prawns turn pink, remove from the heat, stir in the lime juice and ladle into bowls. Garnish with fresh coriander and chilli slices.

TIP: If you can find some enoki mushrooms, what a bonus! Use them instead of button mushrooms.

SERVES 4

I am totally in love with salty-sweet moist gravlax. I normally use a whole side of salmon for this, but because I could eat it every day, whenever I see a small firm freshly cut piece of salmon, I buy it and give it the treatment as quick as I can. Otherwise, out come the soy and wasabi, and the rest is history!

Asian Lemon and Herb-scented Gravlax

- 2 cups coarse salt
- 2 cups white sugar
- zest of 1 lime
- zest of 1 lemon
- 2 stalks lemon grass, very finely chopped
- ½ cup finely chopped mint
- ½ cup finely chopped coriander
- 1 Tbs freshly grated ginger
- 1 tsp white peppercorns, toasted and roughly ground
- 2 tsp dried coriander seeds, toasted and roughly ground
- 1 kg piece Norwegian salmon, from the thick part, with skin on
- fresh herbs, to garnish
- lime wedges, for serving

Mix together the salt and sugar, and set aside. Mix together the lime and lemon zest, lemon grass, mint and coriander, ginger, ground peppercorns and coriander seeds.

Place the salmon skin-side down in a glass dish and rub over the salt and sugar mix. Then rub over the zesty herb mixture, covering it well. Close it up with cling wrap and weigh it down with a couple of cans or even bricks covered with foil.

Leave the salmon to cure in the fridge for about three days; you need to turn it daily and spoon the juices over it every time.

Now it is time to dine on it – yum! Take it out of the dish, wipe off the excess herb mix and slice into thin slivers. Plate it up nicely on a stark white platter and garnish with fresh mint, coriander and a couple of freshly sliced lime cheeks.

SERVES 4 TO 6 AS A STARTER

Palm sugar is one of the most basic ingredients of Thai cuisine. It's gorgeous when it is cooked up and gets all crystallised and lovely and nutty. It tastes like fudge. Sometimes it's light, sometimes it's dark, or hard or soft – divine!

On one of my trips to Thailand I visited a palm sugar factory, which was just an area on the roadside under the shade of coconut palms, with drums full of the coconut flower sap bubbling away over fires. It's boiled until it's gooey and delicious. As a chef I just love discovering the source of the food and where ingredients come from.

Stir-fried Lemon Grass Chicken

LEMON GRASS PASTE

- 2 Tbs crunchy peanut butter
- 2 chillies, seeds and pith removed
- 2 stalks lemon grass, soft centre only
- ½ cup fresh coriander
- 3 Tbs peanut oil
- 1 Tbs fresh lemon juice
- 1 tsp chopped fresh ginger
- 2 cloves garlic
- 2 tsp palm sugar

THE CHICKEN

- 4 chicken breasts, sliced into bite-sized pieces
- oil for stir frying
- 1 cup bean sprouts
- ½ cup chopped mint

Remove the tough outer leaves of the lemon grass and finely slice the soft, scented centre. You can freeze the outer leaves to make a natural room deodoriser.

Place all the ingredients for the paste into a food processor and blitz well.

Mix the paste with the chicken pieces, coating well, cover and let it rest in the fridge. Heat the oil in a large frying pan or wok and cook the chicken with the lemon grass paste till done. Stir in the sprouts and mint, heat through and serve with sticky rice.

SERVES 4

Spicy Basil Pork on Rice Topped with Fried Egg

- 3 Tbs oil
- 1 Tbs crushed garlic
- 2 red chillies, pounded to a paste
- 500 g pork mince
- 2 Tbs fish sauce
- 2 Tbs oyster sauce
- 2 tsp palm sugar or brown sugar
- 1 cup sweet basil
- 2 spring onions with tops, thinly sliced
- 4 eggs
- bowl of cooked rice

Simple and delicious, this dish was cooked for me by a local lady in a grass shack on the banks of a river in Chiang Mai.

Heat the oil in a wok or large frying pan and fry the garlic and chillies until fragrant. Stir in the pork mince and keep it moving in the wok till it is cooked. Add the fish sauce, oyster sauce and sugar, and cook for a minute more. Remove from the heat and stir in the basil and spring onions.

Fry the eggs the way you like them. Spoon some rice into your bowl, top with pork mince and a fried egg, and enjoy!

SERVES 4

I am told that your taste buds have a shelf life of only 10 days, so be kind to them; you don't have much time to make amends if you put less than perfectly fresh ingredients into your mouth. Don't settle for less when you are out shopping for your next meal!

Asian Noodle Slaw

THE DRESSING

- 3 Tbs balsamic vinegar
- 1 Tbs honey
- 2 Tbs dark brown sugar
- 2 Tbs soy sauce
- 2 cloves crushed garlic
- 1 tsp grated fresh ginger
- 2 tsp sesame oil
- ⅔ cup peanut oil
- 1 Tbs chopped fresh coriander
- 1 Tbs chopped fresh mint
- 1 red chilli, chopped (optional)

ASIAN NOODLE SLAW

- 2 cups thinly shredded red cabbage
- 1 cup thinly shredded green cabbage
- 2 cups fresh bean sprouts
- 6 spring onions with tops, thinly sliced
- 1 bunch radish, thinly sliced
- ½ cup toasted sunflower seeds
- ½ cup toasted almonds, roughly chopped
- ½ cup roasted pecan or cashew nuts, roughly chopped
- 2 Tbs toasted sesame seeds
- 100 g Chinese egg noodles, pre-soaked, dried and deep fried

Make the dressing ahead of time so that the flavours can get to know each other. Mix together the first six ingredients until well combined, then whisk in the sesame and peanut oils till well mixed. Stir in the coriander, mint and chilli, and then set the dressing aside to infuse till needed.

All the ingredients for this slaw can be prepared ahead of time and assembled when you are ready to eat. Place them into a large glass bowl, toss with the dressing and serve straight away.

SERVES 4 TO 6

Litchi and Coconut Pana Cotta with Lime Drizzle

PANNA COTTA

- 1½ × 400 g cans coconut milk
- 2 stems lemon grass, bashed to release the flavour
- 1 can litchis, drained, juice reserved and fruit chopped
- 1½ Tbs powdered gelatine
- 1 Tbs castor sugar
- 1 cup fresh cream

LIME DRIZZLE

- ¾ cup water
- ¼ cup lime juice
- ¾ cup sugar
- zest of 2 limes

Place the coconut cream in a saucepan with the lemon grass and litchi juice and bring to a gentle simmer. Cover the saucepan and turn off the heat. Allow the lemon grass to infuse for 30 minutes.

Strain the coconut milk and warm till just hot enough to melt the gelatine. Do not boil. Mix together the gelatine and castor sugar, stir into the hot coconut milk and keep stirring until it dissolves.

Stir in the chopped litchis and fresh cream. Spoon into six wet ramekins and refrigerate for about three hours or until set.

Make the lime drizzle while the panna cotta is setting in the fridge. Place the water, lime juice and sugar into a small saucepan and boil gently till you have a syrupy consistency. Do not stir! Once it has reached the desired consistency, cool slightly and stir in the lime zest. Set aside until you are ready to plate the panna cotta.

Dip the base of each ramekin into warm water and unmould onto a serving plate. Drizzle with the lime syrup and serve.

SERVES 6

Remember to eat up all your dinner unless you want to enrage the Thai God of Rice, a female deity who is said to watch over the people and to make sure that they all have enough to eat. If you waste, you might bring on a famine or even bad luck. I like that way of thinking – we throw so much food away and we should rather share it or cook less.

Crunchy Coconut Bananas

- 4 firm, ripe bananas, peeled
- cake flour, for coating
- 1 cup coarse desiccated coconut
- ½ tsp ground ginger
- 3 Tbs fresh breadcrumbs
- 2 eggs, beaten
- oil for deep frying

Slice the bananas in half lengthways and coat evenly with flour. Mix the coconut, ginger and crumbs together, dip the bananas into the egg and then roll them into the crumb mixture. Chill for 30 minutes.

Heat the oil and deep-fry the bananas in batches till golden and crisp; drain on kitchen paper. Serve with great blobs of vanilla ice cream, honey drizzle and chopped nuts.

SERVES 4

MALAYSIA, BORNEO AND SINGAPORE

Whenever I think of Penang, I think of the time I hired a taxi with my dear friend Antoinette de Chavonnes-Vrugt. The hotel we were staying at recommended a taxi driver to be our personal guide for a day of eating and tasting and discovering. Antoinette is a loveable, crazy redhead but I think she frightened him a little; she kept telling our guide to drive faster, pushing his foot down on the accelerator. When she suggested that he should invite us to his home for tea so that we could meet his family and learn more about the local cuisine from his wife, he said that he lived so far away that it would not be worth the drive.

Ha! He soon changed his tune when he learnt that I was a chef. Before we knew it, we were at his home on the beachfront – actually only a few minutes' drive away.

He had a very humble, tasty-smelling home. His wife had just started to cook lunch for his daughter but sadly we had to turn down an invitation to join them as we were going to have lunch in a shack at the side of the road. (Well, we had a little taste of what Mrs Taxi was cooking; we just couldn't resist it.) While sipping tea so sweet with condensed milk it made my teeth ache, we learnt so much about the Malaysian people.

But before too long, it was time to be on our way. The tin shack was easy enough to find – we just had to follow our noses – and, judging by the bicycles and motorbikes parked alongside, it was popular with the locals. By the time we sat down at a rickety table with dodgy chairs we were ravenous and ready to try everything placed before us. We ordered some freshly squeezed juice and then made our way to a humble buffet set out in chipped, square enamel dishes. It was the most delicious food on earth; glorious fish head curry; fluffy rice; succulent chicken; and spicy beef and noodles. And the seafood dishes! It was hard to believe that this was all possible in such a tiny shack.

That night we had yet another delicious dinner – this time on the Penang beach. With only the beautifully clear star-filled sky to light our meal, we sat at a table placed in the gentle ripples of the shallows, the waves lapping around our ankles to keep us cool and calm.

It might look like a simple dish – well, it is – but oh mama, it is also simply delicious. I eat it at Kuala Lumpur Sentral whenever I arrive in Malaysia, or on the street, or anywhere I can find it. My favourite spot is the Workers' Canteen at KL Sentral. The chicken comes with the rice and broth in bowls on the side. Rice has never tasted so good; it is pure, addictive comfort.

Hainan-style Chicken Rice

DIPPING SAUCE

- 4 Tbs soy sauce
- 1 clove garlic, finely chopped
- 1 spring onion with tops, finely sliced
- 1 tsp sesame oil
- 1 chilli, deseeded and diced
- ½ tsp diced ginger

SAMBAL

- ½ pineapple, peeled, quartered and thinly sliced
- 2 spring onions, thinly sliced
- ½ red onion, thinly sliced
- 1 tsp brown sugar
- 1 red chilli, thinly sliced
- ½ English cucumber, thinly sliced
- salt, to taste
- lime juice, to taste

CHICKEN

- 2 garlic cloves, finely crushed
- 3 spring onions with tops, chopped
- 1 tsp salt
- 1½ cm piece ginger, grated
- 1 whole fresh chicken, about 1.5 kg
- 2 whole cloves
- 8 black peppercorns
- 2 sticks celery, roughly chopped
- 1 tsp sesame oil
- 1 cup long-grain rice

Mix the dipping sauce ingredients together and set aside. Then mix the sambal ingredients together and set aside.

To prepare the chicken, make a paste with the garlic, spring onions, salt and ginger, and rub it into the body and cavity of the chicken. Let it rest in the fridge for an hour.

Place the chicken in a large saucepan and cover with cold water. Add the cloves, peppercorns and celery, and bring to the boil. Turn down the heat and cook gently, simmering and skimming off any froth from the surface.

Simmer for 30 minutes, then turn off the heat and let the chicken rest in the stock for another 30 minutes.

Remove the chicken from the stock, cool it and then rub the skin with the sesame oil. Now cut the chicken in half along the breastbone with a sharp knife. Remove the wings and drumsticks, divide each joint, and cut each breast into three pieces. Cover till needed.

Strain the stock and divide it in half, reserving one half to warm the chicken. Use the remaining stock to cook the rice until it is tender.

Heat the remaining stock in a saucepan and gently warm the chicken pieces in it. Serve the chicken and rice separately, with the sambal on the side. Dip the chicken in the dipping sauce as you eat it.

TIP: I like to remove the skin from the chicken before serving.

SERVES 4 TO 6

Malay Hawker Spiced Fried Chicken

THE PASTE
- 4 large cloves garlic
- 1 medium onion, chopped
- 1 Tbs chopped fresh ginger
- 4 stems lemon grass, inner white part only

THE BATTER
- 2 eggs, beaten
- 1 tsp chilli powder
- 1 tsp ground coriander
- 1 tsp ground cumin
- 1 tsp ground turmeric
- 1 tsp salt
- 1 Tbs sugar
- 4 Tbs cornflour
- 1 Tbs freshly chopped coriander

THE CHICKEN
- 12 chicken pieces
- oil for deep frying

The Colonel can take a back seat to this delicious Malay hawker deep-fried chicken; once you have had it, you've got to have it all the time.

Blend together the ingredients for the paste and then beat the batter ingredients together.

Bring the paste and the batter together, mixing well. Place the chicken pieces into a glass dish, cover with the mixture, and leave to marinate overnight or for at least six hours.

An hour before cooking, remove the chicken from the fridge and let it come to room temperature in a cool place. This facilitates even cooking, so that it is cooked not just on the outside but on the inside too.

Heat the oil in a deep pan and cook the chicken in batches until crisp and golden brown.

TIP: I like to finish the chicken off in the oven just to be sure the inside is cooked through. I heat the oven to 180°C and bake the chicken for about 10 to 12 minutes.

SERVES 4 TO 6

Chinatown Chicken Rolls

- 4 chicken breast fillets
- 2 tsp curry powder
- 200 g prawn meat
- 300 g minced pork or chicken
- 1 Tbs diced carrot
- 2 spring onions with tops, finely chopped
- 2 cloves garlic, grated
- 1 Tbs finely diced celery
- 3 Tbs water chestnuts, diced
- 1 tsp grated ginger
- ½ tsp salt
- 1 tsp sugar
- oil for shallow frying
- cornflour for dusting
- salt and white pepper, to taste

Another Chinatown favourite of mine is chicken wings stuffed with pork and prawns. But I have given it my own twist and made chicken-breast rolls stuffed with this tasty mixture. The wings are fiddly and I prefer to be treated to them when I am next in Chinatown.

Preheat the oven to 180 °C. Slice the chicken breasts in half horizontally and place between two pieces of plastic wrap. Beat them gently to flatten them out.

Mix the curry powder, prawn meat, pork, carrot, spring onions, garlic, celery, water chestnuts, ginger, salt and sugar together.

Divide the filling between the eight chicken portions, pressing it onto three-quarters of the breast. Roll up and secure with a toothpick.

Heat the oil in a large pan. Dust the chicken rolls with cornflour, season with salt and pepper then pan-fry till golden. Transfer to a baking dish and finish off in the oven for 10 minutes.

TIP: Delicious served with sweet chilli sauce mixed with soy sauce, coriander and sliced spring onion.

SERVES 4 TO 6

The Steam Boat – a slow 'Hot Pot' from China

Serving a Malaysian steam boat is sure to bring everyone together around the dinner table. An authentic steam boat is like a Chinese fondue, with hot aromatic broth gently bubbling in a pot over charcoal at the table. Everyone gets to cook their chosen tidbits in it, the food gets scooped up in a spoon with holes, and the broth is consumed at the end. But if you don't have a steam boat then you could just place a pot of broth onto a gas ring. That's really all you need; and some skewers and the best ingredients you can find.

THE STOCK
Chicken stock is an excellent base – two litres should do. Add a few extra bits such as dried shiitake mushrooms (clean, soak and slice them first), spring onions and a pod of star anise. A few slices of fresh ginger, garlic and lemon grass will enhance the flavour and make all the difference.

DUNKING IDEAS
Serve bowls of the freshest vegetables such as bean sprouts, coriander, chilli, Chinese vegetables, mushrooms, chunks of carrot, green beans, roughly chopped spring onions, slices of celery; and of course some tofu, noodles and dumplings; and pork, chicken and beef fillets; and don't forget the fresh prawns, mussels and oysters. I need to stop now! The wonderful thing about a steam boat is that there is space for anything you might want to put into that bubbling pot.

TIP: I like to marinate the meat and seafood so that it is beautifully seasoned before it gets skewered and cooked. Once your food is cooked you can dunk again – this time into a selection of different sauces.

DIPPING IDEAS
Little bowls of dark soy sauce, sesame oil, sweet chilli sauce, hoisin sauce, oyster sauce, plum sauce or a combination that you have mixed yourself, are all delicious for dipping.

SERVES 4

In Malaysia, a Chinese hot pot is known as a 'steam boat'. I love communal eating – it is a wonderful way of socialising and mingling with friends and family. I like the relaxed, leisurely pace of cooking bits and pieces at the table, with lots of little bowls of the freshest ingredients that you dunk into the hot bubbling broth.

That beautiful broth just gets better and more flavourful every time someone dunks a different ingredient into it, and eventually the room is filled with the aromatic steam. You get to drink the broth at the end of the meal – that's worth waiting for, so be sure to leave some space in your tummy for it.

I think that everyone experiences a country's culture and cuisine through their own eyes and mouths. What is charming and quaint to some, may not be clean or neat enough for others.

On one of my trips to Malaysia I decided to take a boat trip to Crab Island, a small island below sea level and home to a charming little fishing village built on stilts. I would imagine that the island got its name because of the abundance of crabs that inhabit the surrounding mangroves. I was told that they really thrive there.

When we arrived on the island, the tide was out and it looked as if the sand was moving from side to side. I could not believe my eyes; the sand was completely covered with crabs scurrying about. I must say, I felt quite dizzy watching them; it felt as if the earth itself was moving. I am sure that the crabs were trying to escape the locals who were doing a fine job of collecting them.

Once we had disembarked from the boat that took us to the island, we made our way into the village along wooden walkways. As we dodged garbage being thrown out of the windows, I noticed that the toilets flushed out from under the huts straight onto the sand beneath them. I made a note to myself to stick to vegetarian dishes that day!

In the little village strings of dried fish were swinging in the breeze from house to house – quite smelly, but very tasty when added to a dish, I was told. I came across a slightly-built, wizened old lady sitting on her haunches with mounds of fresh prawns in front of her, beheading and shelling them at a furious pace. Her frail, tiny fingers worked like a machine. I could not believe how that pile was reduced to heads and shells in no time flat. I looked at all those shells and prayed that they were destined for a rich, tasty broth – I am sure they were; the Chinese never waste a thing. At the sight of that mound of plump little bodies just waiting to be cooked, I very quickly forgot about the garbage and the soiled beach. My mouth was ruling my head yet again!

I was amazed at how many eating houses there were in this little village on stilts, not designed for tourists but for the locals. Needless to say, I succumbed and had a delicious meal of chilli-hot prawns with stir-fried greens and a bowl of sticky rice on the side. It was pure heaven, the prawns so fresh they had been twitching only a few minutes before.

Crab Island-inspired Chilli Prawns

CHILLI SAUCE
- 4 spring onions with tops, finely chopped
- 3 cloves garlic, finely chopped
- 1 Tbs grated fresh ginger
- 3 red chillies
- 2 Tbs rice vinegar
- 2 Tbs tomato sauce
- 2 Tbs water
- 1 tsp sugar
- ½ cup vegetable oil
- 3 Tbs soy sauce
- ½ tsp shrimp paste (optional)
- ¾ tsp sesame oil

PRAWNS
- 1.5 kg medium prawns, shell and head on, deveined and whiskers trimmed
- 2 Tbs chopped fresh coriander
- 2 spring onions with tops, chopped
- 1 Tbs toasted sesame seeds

Blend the sauce ingredients till smooth, and store in a jar in the refrigerator till you need it.

Heat a large wok over medium heat. Add the chilli sauce and simmer until it becomes fragrant; about three to four minutes.

Add the prawns and cook them until they change colour; about five minutes. Taste the sauce and add a little salt if it is needed, then add the chopped coriander and simmer for three more minutes.

Remove from the heat and pile into a deep bowl. Top with the chopped spring onions and sesame seeds, and serve with a bowl of sticky steamed rice.

SERVES 4 TO 6

I have the most wonderful memories of steaming bowls of laksa that I ate in Malaysia at Kuala Lumpur Sentral in a workers' canteen. It was open to the public and as you entered that space, you were enveloped in a sea of wonderful spicy aromas.

Quick and Easy Prawn Laksa

CHILLI PASTE

- 4 stalks fresh lemon grass, tender parts only, finely chopped
- 2 dried chillies, rehydrated in warm water
- 2 fresh red chillies, chopped
- 2.5 cm fresh ginger root, chopped
- ½ tsp shrimp paste
- 3 cloves garlic, chopped
- ½ tsp turmeric
- 1 tsp ground coriander
- 2 Tbs tamarind paste
- 1 Tbs palm sugar or brown sugar

PRAWN LAKSA

- 1 Tbs vegetable oil
- 3 cups chicken stock
- 2 × 400 g cans coconut milk
- 2 tsp fish sauce
- 500 g prawns
- ½ cup fresh coriander sprigs
- lime juice, to taste
- 150 g cooked rice noodles
- ¾ cup fresh bean sprouts
- extra springs of fresh coriander, to garnish

Place all the chilli paste ingredients in a mortar and pound away until it is nice and smooth. If you really have to, you can blend it in a food processor.

To make the laksa, heat the oil in a saucepan, add the spice paste and fry very gently over a low heat, stirring all the time so that you don't burn it. Add a little stock to stop it sticking, and keep stirring for about five minutes to release all that wonderful flavour.

Add the rest of the stock and simmer for 10 minutes, nice and gently. Add the coconut milk and bring it all to a boil. Turn the heat down and stir in the fish sauce, letting the pot simmer for five minutes or so.

Give it a taste and add a little salt if it needs it, add the prawns and cook gently for 10 minutes or until the prawns have turned orange. Stir in the coriander and lime juice.

Get four deep bowls ready, divide up the noodles and prawns into the bowls and ladle in the delicious broth. Top with bean sprouts and a fresh sprig of coriander.

SERVES 4 TO 6

The exciting thing about Malaysian food is that it is derived from multiple ethnic influences – Chinese, Indian, Malay, Thai, Javanese and Sumatran cultures all contribute. Malaysia has a strong oral tradition and the recipes get handed down from mother to daughter. These ladies don't weigh or measure anything when they cook; they just know how it should taste and adjust the flavour as they go.

Sticky Pork Ribs

MARINADE
- 3 cloves garlic, crushed
- 1 Tbs grated ginger
- 1 Tbs hoisin sauce
- 3 Tbs orange marmalade
- 3 Tbs soy sauce
- 2 Tbs balsamic vinegar
- 1 tsp sesame oil
- ¼ tsp ground cloves
- ¼ tsp ground cinnamon
- ¼ tsp ground cumin
- ¼ tsp ground fennel seeds
- ground white pepper
- 2 Tbs peanut oil

PORK RIBS
- 2 pods star anise
- 2 kg meaty pork spare ribs, portioned
- spring onion, to garnish
- fresh coriander, to garnish

Mix the marinade ingredients together and warm gently in a small saucepan. Do not boil. Remove from the heat and set aside.

To prepare the ribs, bring a pot of water with the star anise in it to the boil. Place the ribs into the pot and blanch for six minutes. Transfer the ribs to a large, flat dish and coat well with the marinade. Place in the fridge and leave to marinate for two hours.

Preheat the oven to 200 °C. Roast the ribs for 30 minutes and then reduce the heat to 170 °C, roasting for a further 35 to 40 minutes or until the ribs are tender and soft.

Pile onto a serving platter and garnish with chopped spring onion and coriander.

TIP: Don't let the ribs stick while roasting; add a little hot water to the baking pan.

SERVES 4

Spring Onion and Soy-topped Tofu

- 400 g fresh tofu
- 1½ Tbs vegetable oil
- 2 tsp finely chopped ginger
- 3 spring onions with tops, thinly sliced
- 1 red chilli, sliced
- 1 tsp oyster sauce
- 3 Tbs soy sauce
- 1 tsp sesame oil
- 1 Tbs toasted sesame seeds

Malaysia is a country I love to visit; I love the people and I really love the food. Chinatown is one of my favourite places to eat; there are so many different dishes to choose from. I have a few firm favourites – this delicate, silken tofu is one of them.

Place the tofu into a heat-proof bowl, pour boiling water over it and let it stand for three to four minutes. While the tofu is warming, heat the topping.

Heat the oil till very hot and fry the ginger and spring onions for three minutes, stirring. Add the chilli, oyster sauce, soy sauce and sesame oil, and stir together quickly. Remove from the heat.

Drain the tofu and place onto a warmed plate, pour over the topping and sprinkle with sesame seeds. Serve with stir-fried mushrooms and sticky rice.

SERVES 4

One of the best and most memorable food experiences I had with a tour group was on a trip to Borneo.

The first thing we do when we arrive anywhere is to find the local food markets because that's where you get an immediate sense of a region's ingredients. From what you find there you can make your interpretations of any dish and create your own recipes. Satisfying that urge to get into the kitchen immediately isn't always possible, but in Borneo we made a plan …

We found ourselves in the wet market in Kuching; primitive yet spotless, with concrete slabs piled high with still-twitching prawns of every shape and size just begging to be eaten. I think the group felt the same way I did because they were saying, "Oh my goodness! Can't we cook these?" There we were in a strange country, our mouths screaming for the beautiful fresh produce and we didn't have a kitchen of our own.

We were desperate, so we tried to call our hotel, which was an hour's bus ride away, to see if they could accommodate our yearning to shop and cook. We couldn't get through so we drove all the way back and asked them if we could use their kitchen to cook our own food. We offered to pay them but they turned us down because they were busy preparing a staff party.

By now the group was crazy with lust for those fresh prawns, so something had to be done. We got back on the bus, returned to the market where we bought all the different prawns, herbs, fresh limes, chillies, turmeric, galangal, ginger and garlic – it was all so exciting – and then drove all the way back with our shopping! The hotel kindly supplied some cooked rice, but we still needed something to cook with. Just like our Crazy Stores back home, the 'Two Ringgit' Stores in Borneo had everything we needed; we stocked up on cheap woks and a few melamine bowls.

Back at the hotel, two of the group took the 12 kilos of prawns (which were to be shared between nine of us) and with nail scissors Patsy and her roommate cleaned the entire lot. You should have seen the state of their hands! We stole the dirt bins from the rooms (they were lined with clean paper) to transport the prawns, and all the salt off the tables in the hotel restaurant, and went down to the beach.

Some of the girls got into a fresh-water lagoon and walked up into the forest to gather kindling and driftwood. They brought back enough to keep a bonfire going for three days. We dug a pit into the soft, white beach sand and lined it with some pebbles and bigger boulders from the river. I found two flat stones on which I could grind the spices into three different pastes and then we were all ready to cook. I spent that whole night cooking prawns over the fire, a big silver moon suspended over the calm shimmering South China Sea. What an exquisite meal.

Prawns with Garlic, Chilli and Lemon

PRAWNS
- 2 Tbs olive oil
- 8 cloves garlic, roughly chopped
- 1.5 kg large tiger prawns, deveined, peeled, tails intact
- 1 tsp smoked Spanish paprika
- ½ tsp ground turmeric
- 2 green chillies, deseeded and chopped
- 1 large fresh lemon or lime
- 50 g butter, chopped into blocks
- ½ cup roughly chopped Italian parsley
- ½ cup roughly chopped coriander
- salt and black pepper

RICE
- 50 g butter
- 1 cup chopped spring onions with tops
- ½ cup freshly chopped coriander
- 2 cups precooked long-grain rice
- juice of ½ fresh lemon

The firm pink bodies just burst against your teeth as you bite into the freshest of prawns. They should be eaten with your fingers, and then you can fork up the buttery rice.

Heat the olive oil in a large, non-stick frying pan. Add the garlic, prawns, smoked paprika and turmeric, and stir fry until the prawns start turning pink.

Add the chillies, squeeze the juice of the fresh lemon over the prawns, and remove from the heat. Add the butter, parsley and coriander, season to taste and transfer to a warm dish.

To prepare the rice, add the butter, spring onions and coriander to the pan you used for the prawns, and cook gently for three minutes. Add the rice and lemon juice, and heat through gently.

Pile some rice onto plates and top with the prawns and their juice. A fresh salad of wild rocket leaves would go down a treat with this. Don't gobble those prawns down; savour every mouthful.

TIP: Freeze the prawn shells for a stock or soup.

SERVES 4

It is always a bonus to know someone local when visiting a foreign country. You will get to know where the best food can be had, where all the best markets for fresh produce are located, what to eat and where to shop. In Singapore, the locals seem to eat lots of little bits all day long, and I just love that! When you get shown around by someone in the know, even the fast food tastes slow, just like Mama made it.

South African chef and friend Elsa van der Nest met and married a Chinese Singaporean and settled in Singapore. Talk about good luck and good food; a chef's paradise with all those markets!

On one of my many visits to Singapore, I took my friend Cass Abrahams (also a chef and foodie) to meet up with Elsa for a little culinary adventure around Chinatown. We found ourselves a tiny table on the narrow sidewalk of a very narrow street, with taxis almost touching our backs as they drove past. But the food was so good we soon forgot about the cars.

Being a chef, I always want to visit the kitchens of other chefs and I asked if we could take a peek into the one that was serving all this delicious food. We were invited in and were led into the back of a really tiny room with bamboo cages filled with huge frogs. Their frightened eyes staring at us already got me freaked out, but when we saw the production line, we were done.

There were two youths sitting on midget stools. One, with a very sharp pair of secateurs, took off the frog's head in a swift movement and then passed it on to the other boy, who had the skin off faster than you could blink. Then into the kitchen those poor frogs went, to be cleaned and processed for the deep fryer. I started to cry and they thought I was completely off my rocker.

I have never, ever been able to eat frog again, so let's just stick to crab!

泰
祥
奮

Sometimes when you travel you have to do touristy things, so one day we took ourselves off to Sentosa Island in Singapore where we went off to an amusement park to see a monkey show.

After the show, one of the monkey handlers, a delightfully glorious-looking young man, came over to our group and started chatting to us; I suppose we looked different and interesting. Now, you can buy all kinds of things on the beach there – including spirits – and as some of the girls had bottles of different things in their bags, we decided to go down to the beach for sundowners, and we invited him to join us. The next thing we knew, our beautiful young man sent a monkey up a tree to get a whole lot of coconuts. He whacked the tops off and mixed the drinks with the coconut water inside the shell. While we sipped and chatted, we found out what an interesting young man he was. He'd worked at the zoo in a rehabilitation programme for big cats. His method for keeping them well exercised had been filmed for Animal Planet – he would place cow and chicken blood in their cages at strategic intervals to get them sniffing and running up and down.

There was no way we were going to send this man home. We needed him for the night because we wanted to eat locally. (What did you think we wanted him for?) He admitted that Clark's Quay is quite a touristy destination but said that there was a place there where we would eat the best Singapore chilli crab. We got onto a local bus and made our way there with him. He was absolutely right about that crab. What a wonderful evening!

After the meal, we gave him some dollars, put him in a cab and sent him home. You should have seen the driver's face! And I bet he also had a great story to tell his friends.

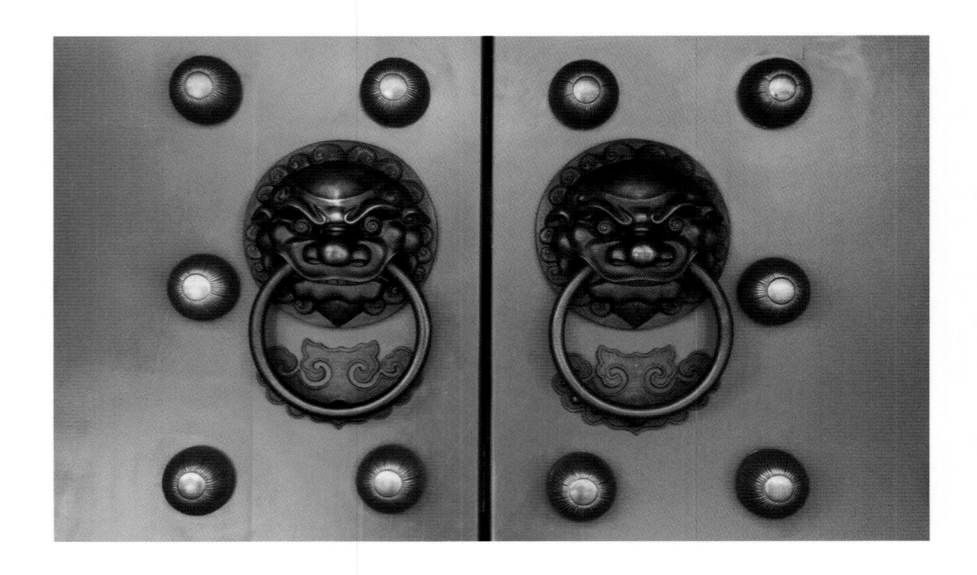

Singapore Chilli Crab

THE CRAB
- 1.5 kg dressed crab (frozen will do)
- 16 prawns, deveined

THE SAUCE
- 3 Tbs peanut oil
- 1 onion, finely diced
- 8 cloves garlic, crushed
- 3 Tbs finely diced ginger
- 3 red chillies, deseeded and sliced
- 4 Tbs black bean sauce
- 2 Tbs sweet chilli sauce
- ½ cup tomato sauce
- 1 tsp tomato purée
- 1 tsp brown sugar
- 2 Tbs rice wine
- 2 tsp salt
- 1 tsp white pepper
- 3 cups chicken stock
- 1 Tbs cornflour mixed with 2 Tbs water
- 2 Tbs dry sherry
- ½ cup chopped coriander
- 3 spring onions with tops, chopped

First prepare the crustaceans. Cut the crab in half lengthways, remove the claws and crack them so that the flavour can leech out. Cut the half crab into three pieces with the legs still attached. Butterfly the prawns in the shell, leaving the head on. Set aside.

To make the chilli sauce, heat the oil in a large saucepan and add the onion, garlic, ginger and chillies; fry till fragrant, stirring all the time. Add all the remaining sauce ingredients except the coriander and spring onion and stir well.

Bring the sauce to the boil and cook for five minutes, then add the crab and cook simmering for eight minutes. Add the prawns and cook for two minutes more.

To serve, stir in the coriander and chopped spring onions, and pile onto a large platter. We ate this with chunks of crusty bread to mop up all that delicious sauce.

TIP: Wear a bib; you really have to get stuck into this dish!

SERVES 4 TO 6

We were a group of women sitting in this beautiful food market in Little India, Singapore. One side of the market was Halaal and the other wasn't, with a table separating the two sections, and there we sat drinking beer and having a good time.

Sitting watching us was a Sikh gentleman, with his traditional turban above thick stubble and a gap-toothed smile. I like making friends with everyone, so I smiled at him. He didn't need any more encouragement than that and he came across to join us, introducing himself as Mr Rajinga Singh.

We got chatting and offered him a drink, and before too long he was a little tipsy. He turned out to be very funny and informative. He showed us the strangest ingredients, like those little fern fronds that come out of the earth before they open fully, that are made into the most amazing salad. He suggested we try the roti – the most enormous roti I have ever seen – with gravy. That's all it was and I have never tasted anything quite so delicious in my life. This is what I love about meeting local people when I travel – they have so much to offer, telling you where to eat the best food.

He invited us to his home, offering to cook us dinner. It wasn't far, he said, only a few minutes by train. We had no intention of going off with him but asked why he couldn't take us in his car. He replied, "No, no. You can't get in my car because you're all very bulky ladies!"

What a cheek! But in honour of our meeting with the otherwise delightful Mr Rajinga Singh, this recipe is for him.

Mushroom Korma for Mr Rajinga Singh

- 2 Tbs sunflower oil
- 1 large onion, finely chopped
- 2 cloves garlic, crushed
- ½ tsp mustard seeds
- 1 tsp grated fresh ginger
- 1 Tbs garam masala
- 1 tsp ground cumin
- 1 tsp ground coriander
- 1 tsp chilli powder
- ½ tsp turmeric
- 1 × 400 g tin coconut cream
- 400 g button mushrooms, halved and lightly fried in butter
- 100 g ground almonds
- 2 Tbs tomato paste
- 1 cup vegetable stock
- salt, to taste
- 200 g steamed green beans, chopped
- 1 red pepper, sliced
- 2 tsp fresh lemon juice
- 1 cup fresh cream
- fresh coriander, chopped

Heat the oil in a large saucepan and slowly fry the onion, garlic and mustard seeds till lightly golden. Add the ginger and all the ground spices, and cook stirring for a minute or two, until they become fragrant. Don't let them burn; add a little water to prevent them catching.

Add the coconut cream and bring to the boil, then stir in the mushrooms, almonds, tomato paste and vegetable stock. Taste for seasoning, then cover the pot and bring to the boil. Remove the lid, reduce the heat and simmer for 10 minutes, giving it a stir every now and then.

Add the beans and peppers, and cook for five minutes or so. Stir in the lemon juice and fresh cream, and garnish with chopped coriander. Serve with rice.

SERVES 4

Singapore Curried Prawns

- 120 g butter
- 4 onions, finely chopped
- 3 cloves garlic, crushed
- 1 tsp toasted cumin seeds
- 1½ tsp ground ginger
- ¼ tsp cayenne pepper
- salt, to taste
- 2 Tbs curry powder
- 2 tomatoes, chopped
- 2½ × 400 g cans coconut milk
- 1 Tbs cornflour
- 1 kg prawns, deveined, eyes off, shell on
- 1 Tbs lemon juice
- 1 Tbs sweet chilli sauce
- fresh coriander, chopped

I just love eating in Singapore. There are so many exciting fusions of cuisines; all those delicious influences from China, Indonesia and India, as well as the dishes that are true to their cultures. Even eating in one of the many food courts guarantees a delicious experience.

Melt the butter in a saucepan and cook the onions down slowly till they are nice and golden, about 10 minutes, giving them a stir every so often. (I have to say, they smell divine while they are cooking.)

Now add the garlic, cumin, ginger, cayenne pepper, salt, curry powder and tomatoes, and cook slowly for another 10 minutes.

Stir the coconut milk and cornflour together and pour it into the tomato mix. Cook for a minute and then add the prawns, lemon juice and sweet chilli sauce.

Cook the prawns till they turn pink, stir in the coriander and then serve right away with steamed rice.

SERVES 4

Chicken, Cucumber and Sprout Salad Dressed with Peanut Sauce

PEANUT SAUCE

- ¼ cup tamarind juice
- ½ red onion, finely chopped
- 2 red chillies, deseeded and finely diced
- 2 Tbs palm sugar or brown sugar
- ⅓ cup crunchy peanut butter
- 4 Tbs dark soy sauce
- ¼ tsp salt
- ¼ cup warm water

CHICKEN SALAD

- 1 Tbs peanut or vegetable oil
- 2 cloves garlic, crushed
- 1 tsp grated ginger
- 4 chicken breasts on the bone, skin on
- salt and ground white pepper, to taste
- 1 English cucumber, peeled
- 300 g very fresh mung bean sprouts
- 2 Tbs chopped coriander
- 3 spring onions with tops, thinly sliced
- 1 carrot, peeled and cut into thin matchsticks
- ½ cup toasted chopped peanuts
- coriander sprigs, for garnishing

This makes a delicious starter or main course on a hot summer's night.

To make the tamarind juice, mix together a tablespoon of tamarind pulp with a quarter cup of water. Let it stand for a little while and then strain.

Whisk all the sauce ingredients together and set aside, allowing the flavours to develop, while you prepare the salad.

Preheat the oven to 180 °C. Mix together the oil, garlic and ginger and rub it all over the chicken. Let it marinate for 60 minutes, then season with salt and pepper. Roast till done; about 30 minutes. Set aside to cool.

Run a fork down the length of the cucumber, salt it and let it sweat for 10 minutes. Rinse off the salt, pat it dry and chill for an hour in the fridge.

Slice the cucumber thinly and toss it together with the sprouts, chopped coriander, spring onions and carrot. Divide the salad between the plates.

Remove the chicken breasts from the bone, slice thinly and place on top of the salad.

Spoon over the peanut sauce, and sprinkle with chopped peanuts and a sprig of fresh coriander. Serve immediately.

SERVES 4 TO 6

VIETNAM

One of my best Vietnamese experiences was the day we all piled into a long boat and went off down the soupy green Mekong River. We were on our way to the home of a local family for a New Year's lunch. Our boatman at the back kept saying, "Okay ladies, little bit to the left, little bit to the right. Forwards! Backwards!" We had to keep the boat balanced because trust me the last thing we wanted was to capsize into that water.

We eventually made it to our destination, scrambling and digging our way up the bank to the home of our hosts, where we received a wonderful warm welcome from the family and their neighbours.

The table was beautifully set and I can't even begin to describe the wonderful aromas – star anise, hints of ginger, garlic. There were bowls brimming with enticing ingredients: flaked slow-braised brisket; the fattest plump pink prawns; fresh mint, coriander, basil and what they call morning glory; swamp cabbage, which gives lots of texture to the food; slivered cucumber and carrots; and a gorgeous dipping sauce. The idea was that the man of the household would show us how to roll all of this into crystal spring rolls, after which we would make our own.

As it was New Year, they offered us chrysanthemum wine, a bitter drink with no alcoholic kick. We reciprocated by offering our own 'New Year wine' from Cape Town: a bottle of whiskey. Needless to say, it had much more of an effect on them than the chrysanthemum wine had on us!

The head man was knocking it back and loving it. After quite a few shots, he took some of the spring roll wrappers, which he soaked in a little warm water, laid them out and proceeded to fill them. While he was doing this, all the attention was on his hands and when I looked down – well! – I have never seen such filthy, grubby fingers or such black nails.

I was heaving deep inside and thinking, "Please don't let him touch my food." Of course he rolled the most perfect, tight little spring roll and offered it to me. I couldn't let him lose face so I said, "I am not worthy of this." So he gave it to a friend sitting next to me – and she didn't love me for that!

He continued to partake of the Cape Town New Year wine for the rest of the meal and when we eventually got down that hill, into the boat and back onto the river, we were telling one another which way to lean to balance the boat. We hadn't realised that the spring roll man and our boatman were one and the same, and he was no longer in any condition to keep himself or us upright.

What I love about Vietnamese food is the balance of flavour, textures and temperature; nothing is too sour or salty, and you can control the heat. All food is consumed to nurture and heal.

Salmon and Prawn Salad

THE DRESSING
- 1 Tbs toasted sesame seeds
- 2 Tbs fresh lime juice
- 1 fat clove garlic, crushed
- ½ tsp grated ginger
- 1 Tbs soy sauce
- 1 Tbs fish sauce
- 2 tsp honey
- 2 tsp wasabi paste
- 1 tsp sesame oil
- 2 Tbs peanut oil

THE SALAD
- 300 g raw, ultra-fresh, middle cut of Norwegian salmon
- 20 deveined prawns, lightly steamed
- butter lettuce
- 200 g mung bean sprouts
- 2 Tbs chopped fresh mint
- 2 Tbs chopped fresh coriander
- 1 medium English cucumber, sliced
- 4 spring onions with tops, sliced at an angle
- 1 ripe firm avocado, peeled and sliced
- sesame seeds, for garnishing

Shake all the dressing ingredients together and taste. Adjust the seasoning if need be, and then set aside until you are ready to dress the salad.

To prepare the salad, slice the salmon thinly and shell the prawns. Arrange the butter lettuce on a large serving platter. Toss the sprouts, mint, coriander, cucumber and half the spring onions together, and scatter them on top of the lettuce.

Arrange the salmon, prawns, avocado and remaining spring onions on the salad and spoon over the dressing. Scatter with sesame seeds and serve immediately.

SERVES 4 TO 6

Deep-fried Prawn Spring Rolls

- 2 Tbs cooking oil
- 2 cm ginger, cut into matchsticks
- 2 carrots, peeled and shredded
- 1 cup chopped celery
- 1 cup shredded red cabbage
- 3 cloves garlic, crushed
- 2 Tbs soy sauce mixed with 1 tsp cornflour
- 1 tsp fish sauce
- 1 tsp brown sugar
- 300 g prawn meat
- ½ cup bean sprouts
- 2 Tbs coriander, chopped
- 1 Tbs mint, chopped
- 12 spring roll wrappers
- 1 egg, beaten
- oil for deep frying
- lime wedges

Heat the oil in a large wok and add the ginger. Fry for half a minute, then add the carrots and celery, stirring for three minutes. Add the cabbage, cook for three minutes, and then add the garlic. Remove from the heat, drain off any liquid and set aside.

Heat the wok and add the soy sauce and cornflour mixture, fish sauce, sugar and prawn meat, and cook till the prawns turn pink. Remove the wok from the heat and stir the vegetables into the prawn meat along with the bean sprouts, coriander and mint.

Drain the filling and divide into 12 portions. Lay the spring roll wrappers out onto a flat surface and cover them with a damp cloth as you work to keep them soft and pliable. With the tips facing towards you, place the filling horizontally at the bottom corner, roll the wrapper up tightly, tucking in the sides as you go, and seal at the end corner with a brush of egg wash. Repeat until you have rolled all of the spring rolls.

Heat the oil in a large pan, and fry the spring rolls in batches until crisp and golden. Drain on paper towels and serve hot with plump wedges of lime.

MAKES 12

The Vietnamese love to wrap and roll and dip their food. These delicious prawn sticks are available on every street corner. They are made from minced prawns pressed onto lemon grass or a sugarcane stick, grilled and then served with a bowl of fresh butter lettuce, mint, coriander, basil and sprouts, with a sweet chilli dipping sauce on the side.

Prawn Sticks

THE SAUCE

- 2 red chillies
- 4 cloves garlic, chopped
- zest of 1 fresh lime
- 1½ Tbs white sugar
- juice of 2 fresh limes
- 4 Tbs fish sauce
- 5 Tbs hot water

PRAWN STICKS

- 1 Tbs vegetable oil
- 1 medium red onion, very finely chopped
- 2 cloves garlic, crushed
- 1 red chilli, finely chopped
- ¼ tsp ground white pepper
- 2 tsp fish sauce
- 2 tsp brown sugar
- 500 g prawn meat
- 1 egg, beaten
- 2 Tbs cornflour
- 8 stalks lemon grass, halved lengthways

THE WRAPS

- a bowl of fresh butter lettuce leaves
- mint
- coriander
- fresh basil
- sprouts

Make the dipping sauce first. Pound together the chillies, garlic, lime zest and sugar, and then stir in the lime juice, fish sauce and hot water. Taste and adjust the seasoning. (I like to pound the sauce ingredients for more flavour extraction.) Set aside until you are ready to serve.

To make the prawn sticks, heat the oil in a saucepan and add the onion, garlic, chilli, pepper, fish sauce and brown sugar, and cook till the onion starts to wilt. Remove from the heat and cool.

Place the onion mix, prawn meat, egg and cornflour into a food processor and blitz to combine. Divide the mixture into 16 balls, press two onto each lemon grass stalk and chill for 30 minutes.

Lightly paint a little oil onto the prawn sticks and cook on a hot grill for five to six minutes; keep turning them as they cook.

Serve the hot prawn sticks along with the fresh herbs and create your own delicious, crunchy wrap. Serve the dipping sauce on the side.

MAKES 8

I learned to make these at the home of a tipsy boatman on the banks of the Mekong River. They are utterly delicious – fresh, crunchy and tasty – and are really easy to make, even though they take a little time to put together.

Get someone to give you a hand soaking the rice paper. The trick is to soak one at a time as they are very delicate, and by the time you have filled one, the next one will be ready to roll with a little help from a friend.

Prawn Crystal Spring Rolls

DIPPING SAUCE

- ½ cup rice vinegar
- ¼ cup boiling water
- ½ cup castor sugar
- 1 Tbs fish sauce
- 2 small chillies, chopped
- 1 Tbs chopped fresh coriander
- 1 tsp sesame oil
- 1 Tbs finely diced fresh cucumber

SPRING ROLLS

- 1 cup finely shredded red cabbage
- 1 large carrot, peeled and thinly julienned
- 1 cup freshest bean sprouts
- 1 medium English cucumber, julienned
- 24 large fresh mint leaves
- 24 fresh basil leaves
- 12 coriander sprigs
- 24 prawns, deveined, lightly steamed and shelled
- 12 butter lettuce leaves
- 12 dried rice paper rounds

Make the dipping sauce first. Place the vinegar and water in a saucepan over medium heat and add the sugar, stirring to dissolve. Bring to the boil and let it bubble away for a few minutes. Remove from the heat and stir in the fish sauce and chillies. Stir in the chopped coriander, sesame oil and diced cucumber when cool and set aside.

To make the spring rolls, place one rice paper round at a time in a bowl of warm water to soften slightly. Remove to a flat surface and place a little red cabbage, carrot, a few bean sprouts and some cucumber in the centre of the rice paper, top with two fresh mint and basil leaves and a sprig of coriander. Now top with two prawns and a lettuce leaf – if the leaves are too big, trim them to size.

Fold in the sides of the rice paper and gently roll up nice and tight. Do the same with the remaining rounds of rice paper. Pack onto a tray with enough space between them so they don't stick together, and cover with a damp clean cloth.

When you are ready to serve, slice the rolls in half diagonally, place on a plate and serve with dipping sauce.

I sometimes make these with shredded duck breast, rare thinly sliced beef fillet, shredded chicken breasts, or even leave out the meat and go vegetarian. If you can lay your hands on some Vietnamese mint please add a leaf to your roll.

TIP: You can make these up to two hours ahead – just cover them with a clean damp cloth to prevent them from drying out!

MAKES 12

When I first arrived in Vietnam I didn't know what to expect, but I had an idea of what I wanted to taste because I had tried Vietnamese food before. I was curious though – would it taste better, or just different? Oh boy, it was far better than anything I could ever have imagined!

Stuffed Calamari

- 12 medium-sized tubes of calamari
- 1 Tbs peanut oil
- 1 Tbs finely chopped fresh ginger
- 3 cloves garlic, crushed
- 3 stalks lemon grass, centres only, finely chopped
- 200 g pork or chicken mince
- 1 large chilli, chopped
- 2 tsp brown sugar
- 1 Tbs fish sauce
- ½ tsp ground white pepper
- 100 g chopped mushrooms
- 4 spring onions with tops, finely chopped
- ½ cup finely chopped green beans
- 1 cup prawn meat, chopped
- ¾ cup cooked rice noodles, chopped into medium-sized lengths
- 2 Tbs chopped fresh basil
- 2 Tbs chopped fresh coriander
- oil for deep frying
- cornflour, for dusting
- 2 egg whites, lightly beaten

Give the calamari a good clean and peel off the thin membrane covering the tubes.

Heat the oil in a large frying pan and add the ginger, garlic and lemon grass. Cook stirring for 30 seconds. Now stir in the pork, chilli and brown sugar, and cook stirring for two minutes.

Add the fish sauce, pepper and mushrooms, and cook for two minutes. Then add the spring onions, green beans and prawn meat, and cook till the prawns are almost pink.

Stir in the noodles, and add the basil and coriander. Remove from the heat and cool the mixture.

Stuff the calamari tubes till two-thirds full, fold over the top and secure with toothpicks.

Heat the oil in a pan suitable for deep frying. Toss the calamari in cornflour and then into egg white, and deep-fry in batches till golden and firm to the touch. Drain on paper towels and keep warm.

When all the calamari has been cooked, serve immediately with sweet tamarind sauce (see opposite for recipe) and a bowl of mixed lettuce leaves and fresh mint, dill, coriander and basil.

TIP: Keep the outer pieces of lemon grass and add them to oil for deep frying to scent it; remove it when you can smell its fragrance.

SERVES 6

Sweet Chilli and Cucumber Dipping Sauce

- 1 Tbs cooking oil
- 1 thumb-sized piece of peeled ginger, cut into matchsticks
- ½ cup white sugar
- ½ cup rice wine vinegar
- ½ cup water
- 2 cloves garlic, diced or sliced
- 3 red chillies, cut into thin strips
- ½ cup diced cucumber, with skin on

Heat the oil in a saucepan, add the ginger and cook for 30 seconds. Stir in the sugar and cook for another 30 seconds, stirring all the time. Add the vinegar and water, and cook slowly until slightly syrupy. Stir in the garlic and chillies and remove from the heat.

Cool and stir in the cucumber. Serve with all things that love to be dipped and dunked!

MAKES ABOUT 1½ CUPS

Tamarind Dipping Sauce

- 100 g tamarind pulp soaked in 1½ cups warm water
- 2 Tbs rice vinegar
- 8 Tbs brown sugar
- 1 red chilli, deseeded and finely chopped
- 4 cloves garlic, crushed
- 2 spring onions with tops, chopped
- 8 Tbs fish sauce
- 6 Tbs fresh lime juice
- zest of 2 limes

Tamarind is used all over Southeast Asia and it has a wonderfully fruity, sweet-and-sour flavour. It is also a great natural laxative: I can vouch for that after munching away at a couple of pods too many while on a trip in Thailand!

Place all the ingredients, except the fish sauce, lime juice and zest, into a saucepan and bring gently to a boil. Remove from the heat and push through a sieve.

Stir in the fish sauce, lime juice and zest, taste and balance the flavours. This sauce is especially good served with beef, chicken and lamb dishes, and with prawns.

MAKES ABOUT 2 CUPS

Stuffed Pork Chops with Grilled Pineapple on a Stick

THE FILLING
- 1 Tbs oil
- 3 spring onions with tops, chopped
- 2 stems lemon grass, tender part only, finely chopped
- 2 cloves garlic, thinly sliced
- zest of 1 lime
- 2 tsp fish sauce
- 250 g prawn meat, roughly chopped
- ½ cup fresh breadcrumbs
- 2 Tbs chopped fresh coriander

THE CHOPS
- 4 thick pork loin chops, rind removed and fat trimmed
- salt
- ground white pepper
- cornflour
- 2 eggs, beaten
- 2 cups fresh breadcrumbs or panko crumbs
- oil for shallow frying

PINEAPPLE SATAY
- 1 tsp sesame oil
- 1 tsp vegetable oil
- 1 tsp white sugar
- 5 thick slices of sweet ripe pineapple, peeled and cut into chunks

THE SYRUP
- ½ cup castor sugar
- ½ cup water
- 2 tsp rice wine vinegar
- 2 red chillies, deseeded and thinly sliced
- zest of 1 lime
- 8 mint leaves, rolled and thinly sliced

Start by getting the filling ready. Heat the oil in a pan, add the spring onions, lemon grass, garlic and lime zest, and wilt them for a minute to release their flavours. Stir in the fish sauce and remove from the heat.

Now place the prawn meat, breadcrumbs, fresh coriander and contents of the pan into a glass bowl. Mix together well and divide into four portions.

Preheat the oven to 180 °C. Using a very sharp, thin-bladed knife, make a slit in each chop, going in from the fat side, and open a pocket towards the bone. Stuff a quarter of the prawn filling into the cavity and press it closed.

Season the chops with salt and pepper, dust with cornflour, dip into the egg and press into the crumbs, taking care to double-crumb the cut edge. Chill till needed, only taking them from the refrigerator 30 minutes before cooking.

Heat the oil and fry the chops till almost golden brown, remove from the oil and place onto an oven tray. Bake for 10 to 15 minutes.

While the chops are cooking, make the pineapple satay and the chilli syrup. Mix the oil with the sugar, add the pineapple, toss to coat and thread onto four wooden skewers. Heat a grill pan and grill for a few minutes on each side.

To make the syrup, place the castor sugar, water and vinegar into a small saucepan, and stir till the sugar dissolves. Add the chillies and simmer for about five minutes so that the heat of the chilli can infuse the syrup. Remove from the heat and stir in the lime zest and mint. Pour into a bowl and set aside till needed.

When the chops are cooked through, remove from the oven and serve immediately with the pineapple satay and chilli syrup.

SERVES 4

Steamed Pork Dumplings with Lettuce Wraps and Dipping Sauce

PORK DUMPLINGS

- 800 g pork mince
- 225 g canned water chestnuts
- 3 spring onions with tops, finely chopped
- 2 cloves garlic, crushed
- 1 tsp grated ginger
- 2 tsp sesame oil
- 1 Tbs soy sauce
- 1 Tbs coriander, chopped
- 2 stems lemon grass, soft inner part only, finely chopped
- 1 red chilli, deseeded, finely chopped
- ¼ tsp ground white pepper

CARAMEL DIPPING SAUCE

- 4 Tbs brown sugar
- 2 Tbs warm water
- 4 Tbs fish sauce
- 6 Tbs lime juice
- zest of 2 limes
- 1 chilli, sliced
- ½ tsp sesame oil
- 1 clove garlic, finely chopped

LETTUCE WRAPS

- large bowl butter lettuce leaves
- fresh basil
- fresh mint
- fresh coriander
- sprouts
- cucumber sticks

Place the pork in a bowl. Drain the water chestnuts, chop finely and stir into the pork. Add the spring onions, garlic, ginger, sesame oil, soy sauce, coriander, lemon grass, chilli and pepper. Mix together well.

Roll into balls slightly bigger than a walnut or small plum. Line a bamboo steamer or colander with cabbage or lettuce leaves, set it over a steaming pot of water, place the pork balls onto that and steam for about 20 to 25 minutes.

While the dumplings are steaming, make the dipping sauce. Place the sugar and water in a small saucepan, and heat it gently until it starts to turn a golden caramel colour. Transfer to a bowl and add the remaining sauce ingredients. Mix together, taste, and adjust seasoning. Keep the caramel warm over a pot of hot water.

Now eat it like this: wrap a pork dumpling with some herbs, sprouts and cucumber in a lettuce leaf, drizzle or dip with sauce and enjoy!

SERVES 4

I love the textures and flavours of this salad. I ate it in Thailand and Vietnam and can't get enough of it. Plant a banana tree and use the blossom – it is worth it! If you can't find banana blossom then use shredded carrots and cucumber to replace it.

Banana Blossom Salad

THE DRESSING
- 4 cloves garlic, peeled
- 1 tsp freshly grated ginger
- 3 red chillies (less if you can't take the heat)
- 3 Tbs palm sugar
- 1 Tbs good-quality sweet chilli sauce
- 1 Tbs crunchy peanut butter
- 2 tsp fish sauce
- 2 Tbs rice wine vinegar
- ¾ cup fresh lime juice

THE SALAD
- 1 fresh banana blossom
- juice of 2 lemons
- 200 g fresh bean sprouts
- 1 cup fresh coriander, roughly chopped
- 1 cup fresh mint, roughly chopped
- 1 cup fresh basil, roughly torn
- 1 shredded Granny Smith apple
- 1 cup shredded green papaya or green mango
- 1½ cups raw peanuts, toasted in a pan
- 2 cups peeled prawns, lightly steamed

I like to make the dressing up front and let it stand a bit so that the ingredients can get to know each other.

Pound together the garlic, ginger and chillies till smooth. Add the palm sugar, sweet chilli sauce and peanut butter, and stir in well to combine. Add the remaining dressing ingredients, mixing well.

You can adjust the sweet and sour taste to your liking once the dressing is made.

It's important to put this salad together just before serving, because the banana blossom will turn brown quite fast. When you shred it, toss it in the lemon juice straight away.

Using a sharp knife, remove the four outer leaves of the banana blossom – you can throw them away or use them as a dish for serving the salad. Cut off the top and the bottom of the blossom. Now, slicing crosswise from the top, shred as thinly as possible and place immediately in a bowl of water with the lemon juice. If you come across any baby bananas, get rid of them.

Leave the shredded banana blossom in the water for 30 minutes, then drain and dry it just before the salad is ready to be served.

Now fling all the remaining salad ingredients together, scatter over the banana blossom, dress it up with the dressing, giving it a good toss to coat, pile onto a platter and be transported to heaven.

Place the platter in the middle of the table and let everyone tuck in, or you can plate up individual servings if you prefer.

TIP: Add some shredded duck breast instead of prawns, if you like. Oh, Mama!

SERVES 6

One of my most vivid memories of Vietnam is of two young girls sitting on their haunches in a broth house kitchen with an enamel basin the size of a small fishpond between them. It was piled high with steaming fragrant beef, flavoured with star anise, cloves, ginger, garlic, onions, peppercorns, cardamom and cinnamon. They were removing big chunks of fat from the meat before shredding it to add to the noodle broth we were about to eat, served with huge bowls of herbs, sprouts and greens I couldn't identify. It's not so much the beef that's the star of the show but the broth itself. As the steaming bowl was placed in front of me I couldn't help inhaling deeply. I just had to fill my body with that delicious aroma.

Pho

THE BROTH
- 500g oxtail
- 1kg beef shin
- 4cm peeled ginger, thickly sliced and bashed
- 5 cloves garlic with skin on, bashed
- 3 medium onions in their skin, quartered
- 4 stalks celery, roughly chopped
- 2 dried cloves
- 1 cinnamon stick
- 2 split cardamom pods
- 10 peppercorns
- 2 star anise pods
- 4 litres cold water

BITS FOR THE BOWL
- 200g rice noodles, cooked
- 300g fresh bean sprouts
- 6 spring onions, thinly sliced
- 6 fresh chillies, thinly sliced
- sliced-up beef, from the broth
- fish sauce, to taste
- 6 lime wedges
- a large bowl of mixed herbs (fresh basil, mint, coriander)
- fresh soup celery leaves, chopped

Place all the broth ingredients in a large soup pot, cover with the water and bring gently to the boil. Skim the surface to remove the scum that rises to the surface.

Turn down the heat and simmer gently with the lid on for one-and-a-half hours until the meat is really soft and tender. Remove the lid and simmer for another one-and-a-half hours; the stock should just tremble.

Remove the meat from the broth, slice it up and put the slices in a serving bowl. Strain the broth, pour it into a clean pot and fling in a couple of ice blocks to gather up any floating fat. Remove the fatty ice blocks and reheat the broth by simmering for 20 minutes with the lid off.

Place all the bits for the bottom of the soup bowls in little dishes on the table and let everyone help themselves. Place some noodles at the bottom of each soup bowl, then some sprouts, spring onions, chillies and beef. Cover with hot broth, season with fish sauce and a squeeze of lime, and add the herbs of your choice. Happy slurping!

TIP: Skim the stock all the time and do not boil after the initial boiling stage, otherwise you will have a tasty but cloudy stock. I make this the day before I need it and once it has cooled completely put it in the refrigerator – this makes it easy to remove any fat.

SERVES 6

Vietnamese Caramelised Beef

- 4 Tbs brown sugar
- 2 Tbs warm water
- 1 tsp lime juice
- 3 Tbs peanut oil
- 1 kg fillet, sirloin or rump, cut into strips
- 1.5 cm fresh ginger, grated
- 2 cloves garlic, chopped
- 4 Tbs fish sauce
- salt and ground white pepper, to taste
- 1 stem lemon grass, tender inner part, finely chopped
- handful fresh coriander, chopped
- 3 spring onions with tops, finely chopped
- 1 small red chilli, chopped

Place the sugar and water into a small saucepan, and heat it gently until it starts to turn a golden caramel colour. Transfer to a heat-proof bowl. Stir in the lime juice and keep the caramel warm over a pot of hot water.

Get the oil nice and hot in a wok or large frying pan and brown the steak, ginger and garlic. Stir in the caramel and fish sauce, and season with salt and pepper. Stir fry for about six minutes, making sure that it doesn't catch.

Remove from the heat and pile onto a platter. Scatter with lemon grass, coriander, spring onion and chilli. Serve with a bowl of steamed sticky rice.

SERVES 4

I have eaten chicken satay with these flavours on the street in Ho Chi Minh City – I just hope I have remembered all of them. Here I use baby chickens and serve the dish as a main course.

Honeyed Lemon Grass Chicken

THE SAUCE
- 5 Tbs honey
- 1 Tbs brown sugar
- 3 Tbs chopped ginger
- 6 cloves garlic
- ¾ tsp white pepper
- 3 whole stalks lemon grass, chopped
- 1 Tbs sesame oil
- 1 Tbs fish sauce
- ½ cup soy sauce
- zest and juice of 2 oranges
- ½ cup hot water
- 1 star anise

- 4 spatchcocked baby chickens

Place all the sauce ingredients in a saucepan and bring to the boil. Remove from the heat, cool and then liquidise till smooth.

Lay the chickens out in a large dish and rub on the sauce. Transfer the birds into zip lock plastic bags, spoon over any leftover sauce and marinate overnight in the fridge.

Preheat the oven to 220 °C. Place the chickens breast-side up in a large roasting pan and roast for 10 minutes. Turn the oven down to 200 °C and roast, basting as you go, for 20 to 25 minutes, or till the juices run clear and the legs move easily when wiggled.

Serve with sticky rice and a salad of mint, sweet basil, sprouts, sliced radishes and thinly slivered red onion.

TIP: The colours of the salad are so beautiful – I like to serve this dish on a pale turquoise plate.

SERVES 4

Chilli Beef on Noodle Cake with Pickle

PICKLED CUCUMBER
- 1 large English cucumber, peeled and thinly sliced
- 1 Tbs roughly chopped mint
- 2 spring onions with tops, thinly sliced
- ½ tsp white sugar
- ½ tsp salt
- ½ tsp ground white pepper
- zest of 1 lime
- juice of 1 lime
- 1 Tbs peanut oil
- 1 Tbs rice wine vinegar

CHILLI BEEF
- 4 Tbs oil
- 500 g sirloin, cut into thin strips
- 4 cloves garlic, finely chopped
- 1 Tbs curry powder
- ½ tsp crushed dry chillies
- 4 Tbs cornflour
- 2 tsp fish sauce
- 1 tsp brown sugar
- 2 stalks lemon grass, minced
- oil for deep frying
- toasted sesame seeds, for garnishing

NOODLE CAKE
- 300 g cooked egg noodles
- 2 Tbs chopped coriander
- 2 tsp fish sauce
- 1 tsp sesame oil
- ground white pepper, to taste
- 1 tsp brown sugar
- 1 Tbs soy sauce
- 2 Tbs peanut oil

Make the pickle first. Place the sliced cucumber into a bowl, and sprinkle over the remaining ingredients. Using your hands, toss together well and pile onto a serving plate. Set aside while you prepare the beef.

Now make the chilli beef. Place the oil, beef, garlic, curry powder, crushed chillies, cornflour, fish sauce, sugar and lemon grass in a bowl, and mix together well to coat the beef.

Deep fry the beef in batches, drain on paper towels and keep warm while you prepare the noodle cake.

To make the noodle cakes, place the cooked noodles into a bowl with all the remaining ingredients, except the two tablespoons of peanut oil. Toss together with two forks, ensuring that the noodles are well coated. Divide the noodles into four portions.

Heat the peanut oil in a pan, press one portion of noodles into the base and fry till golden. Turn the noodle cake over, brown the other side and then drain on paper towel. Repeat with the remaining noodle portions.

Place a noodle cake onto a plate and top with some chilli beef and pickled cucumber. Garnish with a scattering of toasted sesame seeds. Serve with extra cucumber on the side.

SERVES 4

INDEX

SUNBIRD PUBLISHERS

First Published in 2013

Sunbird Publishers
The illustrated imprint of Jonathan Ball Publishers
(A division of Media24 Pty Ltd)
P O Box 6836
Roggebaai 8012
Cape Town, South Africa

www.sunbirdpublishers.co.za

Registration number: 1984/003543/07

www.jennymorris.co.uk
www.jennymorris.co.za
www.gigglinggourmet.com

Design and typesetting by MR Design
Cover design by MR Design
Editing and project management by Michelle Marlin
Proofreading by Kathleen Sutton
Food photography by Danie Nel Photography
Food styling by Caroline Gardner
Food assistant Caro Alberts
Reproduction by Resolution Colour, Cape Town
Printed and bound by Craft Print International Ltd, Singapore

ISBN 978-1-920289-75-1